W9-ARG-624

Historical Association Studies

The Counter-Reformation

Historical Association Studies
General Editors: Roger Mettam and James Shields

The Historical Association, 59a Kennington Park Road,
London SE11 4JH

The Counter-Reformation

N. S. DAVIDSON

Basil Blackwell

Copyright © N. S. Davidson 1987

First published 1987

Basil Blackwell Ltd
108 Cowley Road, Oxford, OX4 1JF, UK

Basil Blackwell Inc,
432 Park Avenue South, Suite 1503
New York, NY 10016, USA

British Library Cataloguing in Publication Data

Davidson, N.S.
    The Counter-Reformation.——
    (Historical Association studies)
    1. Counter-Reformation
    I. Title   II. Series
    270.6   BR430
    ISBN   0-631-14888-4

Library of Congress Cataloging in Publication Data

Davidson, N. S. (Nicholas S.), 1952–
    The Counter-Reformation.

    (Historical Association studies)
    Bibliography: p.
    Includes index.
    1. Counter-Reformation. I. Title. II. Series.
BR430.D38   1987   282'.09'031   87–9334
ISBN 0–631–14888–4 (pbk.)

Typeset in 11 on 12 pt Baskerville
by Photographics, Honiton, Devon
Printed in Great Britain by Page Bros, Norwich

To the memory of
Campbell and Joyce

Contents

Introduction

The concept of a 'Counter-Reformation' was first developed in the nineteenth century, when Protestant historians needed a label for Catholic resistance to the Reformation. The phrase they selected – *Gegenreformation* in German, Counter- or even Anti-Reformation in English – clearly implied that a new era had opened in Catholic history in 1517. The Counter-Reformation, they believed, began as a reaction to Luther's protest in that year against indulgences, and then continued until the Peace of Westphalia in 1648: 'By this peace', wrote Leopold von Ranke in the 1830s, 'a termination was at last put to the grand struggle between protestants and catholics' (Ranke, 1842, p. 274). But Catholic historians, who believe that the Church in the sixteenth and seventeenth centuries was animated by more than a response to Protestantism, have often preferred the term 'Catholic Reformation'. They have argued that reform in the Church actually predated Luther, and survived the Peace of Westphalia, to inspire a revived spirituality in the eighteenth century and beyond.

Early modern Catholicism has received a good deal of historical attention in recent years, and the assumptions that lay behind the concept of a Counter-Reformation are no longer acceptable. The work of scholars

1

such as Outram Evennett, Jean Delumeau and John Bossy has demonstrated that reform in the Catholic Church was not just the reaction of an institution under threat, and some historians would now like to abandon the term Counter-Reformation altogether. It is also clear, however, that the history of Catholicism was redirected as a result of the Reformation, and that change in the Catholic Church did not take place in blithe isolation from events in northern Europe. Neither the term Counter-Reformation nor Catholic Reformation is therefore entirely satisfactory. But 'The Counter-Reformation' seems to have acquired such a wide currency in historical writing that it would be unwise to replace it now; we can retain the label without adopting its early implications.

Despite the quality and volume of modern research, however, the Counter-Reformation still remains difficult to grasp. It seems at first sight a leaden subject, cheerless, uncongenial and insignificant beside the large themes and high drama of the Reformation. The history of Protestantism is marked by imposing personalities and striking events – Luther, Calvin, the Peasants' War, the French Wars of Religion. There is nothing so rousing in the history of Catholicism, and it is consequently much less familiar to the non-expert. To provide a focus for the Counter-Reformation, we have to experiment with a rather different kind of approach.

The Reformation was fired by Luther's conviction that Rome had abandoned the truth of the Gospel, and fuelled by his contemporaries' hostility to corruption in the Church. We should therefore begin the analysis of the Counter-Reformation with a chapter on *Catholic doctrine* (chapter 1), before and after the Council of Trent, and then examine the impact of the Council's rulings on *the clergy* (chapter 2). Trent's decisions on doctrine and discipline provided a framework for the 'new

2

Catholicism' of the Counter-Reformation, headed by a revived papacy, and implemented by bishops, priests and the religious orders. This story of the motives and methods of Catholic reform has often been studied before; but it must be balanced by an examination of *the laity* (chapter 3), whose understanding of religion was not always in line with either the old or the new Catholicism. Yet the most arresting feature of Church history in this period is, perhaps, the growth of Catholic belief beyond Europe; so the next chapter should be on *missions* (chapter 4) – to the Protestants first, and then to the non-Christian and pagan populations of America, Africa and Asia.

The Church's attempts to control and increase its members, by persuasion or force, lead us to the heart of Catholic history in this period, and so finally to an assessment of *the impact of the Counter-Reformation* (chapter 5) on society in Europe and abroad. It is here, in the relationship of Church and people, that the significance of Catholic history in the sixteenth and seventeenth centuries can be most readily appreciated.

1 Catholic Doctrine and the Council of Trent

The fierce doctrinal differences which divided Protestants from Catholics in the sixteenth century can easily blind us to the fact that on most theological matters the Reformation and the Counter-Reformation were in agreement. In 1500, most Christians in Western Europe would have accepted the traditional doctrine of the Trinity – the belief that God exists in One Substance but Three Persons: Father, Son and Holy Spirit. God the Father had created all things. God the Son had become man in the Incarnation as Jesus of Nazareth, born of Mary, crucified by Pontius Pilate and raised from the dead. God the Holy Spirit had inspired the Scriptures, and was still at work among men and women in the world. They would have accepted too the scriptural teaching that the first man, Adam, had rebelled against God, and that all Adam's descendants had inherited from him that propensity to disobedience which is called Original Sin. But they would also have believed that Jesus' suffering and death on the cross, his Passion, had made possible a new reconciliation between man and God.

The Reformation controversies were concerned not so much with the content of this shared theological inheritance, as with its mechanisms, and in particular with the process through which sinners could be reconciled with God. It is often assumed that the doctrines associated with Protestantism were first enunciated by Martin Luther, but Luther's thought can in fact be located in a long tradition of discussion and debate within the Church. To understand the Protestant doctrinal challenge, and the Catholic response, we must therefore first examine some of the characteristics of religious life in the later Middle Ages.

The pre-Reformation Church was by no means the devotional desert condemned by its Protestant critics. One of the more influential revivals in the fourteenth and fifteenth centuries was the *Devotio Moderna*, which originated in the Low Countries. Its most celebrated product is probably *The Imitation of Christ*, which first appeared in 1418 and is usually attributed to Thomas à Kempis. The purpose of this book was to develop its reader's inner life by encouraging him to enter a more personal relationship with Christ. Its main emphasis was therefore on religion as a subjective experience, though it contained no suggestion of any disloyalty to the Church as an institution. The *Devotio Moderna* was not, of course, the only revival of this period, but the interests of Thomas à Kempis were echoed by many other devotional writers. Intuition was valued above argument, and work below prayer and meditation. Richard Rolle, a hermit from Yorkshire, had no doubt in 1343 that contemplation was superior to action: 'a man is not more holy or excellent because of the outward deeds he performs. For God who looks on the heart rewards the will rather than the deed ... Therefore the active life is rightly put second, and the contemplative preferred' (Rolle, 1971, p. 111).

Two features of this approach are worth noting here. The first is that in his relationship with man, God is

5

given the initiative: a Christian should be a passive recipient, abandoned to the will of God. As the author of the anonymous fourteenth-century *Cloud of Unknowing* explained, 'this is the work of God alone, deliberately wrought in whatever soul he chooses, irrespective of the merits of that particular soul.' The second is that the consequence of this subjective experience was often a desire to withdraw still further from the world: 'as far as possible avoid the company of men', advised Thomas à Kempis.

In this introspective atmosphere, preoccupied with the cultivation of a personal spirituality, the nature and significance of sin and grace were popular subjects for theological discussion. 'Sin' can be defined as a deliberate act of disobedience to the known will of God; a rather more precise concept than 'immorality', it directly concerns only God and the sinner. 'Grace' is God's assistance, which can help the sinner avoid sin. When an individual is brought back from sin to obedience, he or she is said to experience *justification*. At first sight these theological concepts about a private religious experience seem relatively simple, but they became the focus for almost every major doctrinal argument of the Reformation period, and they form the background to Luther's early doctrinal writings.

Luther believed that the effect of Original Sin on the human soul was so drastic that no individual could by an act of will freely perform any virtuous act. By our very nature, we are opposed to everything God wills, and it is as a consequence impossible for us to experience justification voluntarily. Only the free gift of God's grace can initiate the process of justification. And even after we have been justified by God, Luther believed that we are still subject to the desire to sin. We cannot therefore merit salvation: that too must be the gift of God. This, Luther believed, was the teaching of the Bible, which

6

he accepted as the sole authoritative source of revelation.

Luther began to formulate his teaching on justification after his celebrated 'Tower Experience', which probably took place in 1513 or 1514; but he was not the only, nor the first, theologian to adopt these doctrines. In Spain, Pedro Ruiz de Alcaraz was teaching the same sort of theology from 1510. And in 1511, Gasparo Contarini, a Venetian patrician, had a similar 'experience' on the island of S. Giorgio Maggiore at Easter. Much of what he believed was, indeed, almost indistinguishable from the teaching of Luther, as he sometimes acknowledged himself. He summarized his doctrine of justification in a letter of 1523:

> I have truly come to the firm conclusion (which, however, I had first read and experienced for myself) that no one can at any time justify himself through his works or purge his mind of its inclinations. One must turn to the divine grace obtained through faith in Jesus Christ, as St Paul says ... We must justify ourselves through the righteousness of another, that is, of Christ, and when we join ourselves to him, his righteousness is made ours. (Fenton, 1972, pp. 10–11)

Contarini's belief that we cannot by an act of free will eliminate our inherently sinful inclinations, his consequent assurance in justification by the grace of God, even his reliance on the authority of Scripture – these all come close to Luther's theological understanding. Yet Contarini and Alcaraz did not influence Luther: they simply shared a common religious experience, which they described in comparable ways. And we can trace the same line of thought well before the sixteenth century – in the work of the fourteenth-century philosopher Gregory of Rimini, for example, and ultimately in the New Testament theology of St Paul. By the early sixteenth century, however, it had become a dominant theme, reinforced by an intense academic investigation of the Bible and the early Christian Fathers, especially St Augustine.

This pre-Reformation interest in the problem of justification was not necessarily heretical, or unorthodox. The Catholic authorities had not previously made a clear doctrinal statement on the matter, and a commitment to the Pauline tradition did not involve any inevitable hostility to the Church: Gasparo Contarini, whose experience of justification predated Luther's, became a cardinal in 1535. But Luther's development of these doctrines brought him, quite logically, to reject the theological necessity for an institutional Church. If an individual can be justified by the free gift of God, there is simply no need for a Church, no need for the papacy or the priesthood, for sacraments, saints and indulgences. Luther and his followers in Germany were therefore led into schism, and formally separated from Rome. By 1540 it had become clear that sympathy for the Reformation was growing south of the Alps as well, and the Church authorities became increasingly fearful of the risk of schism in Italian cities like Lucca, Milan, Modena, Naples and Venice. The Catholic clergy could do little to prevent it, for they were still uncertain what they should teach. It was therefore essential to provide an authoritative statement on the doctrines in debate.

On 5 April 1541, a theological conference was opened at Regensburg. The Protestant theologians included Melanchthon and Bucer; the Catholics were Eck, Pflug and Gropper. Contarini was papal legate. They were not empowered to discuss administrative reform, but they did reach agreement among themselves on the doctrine of justification. On 13 May, however, the conference collapsed in disagreement over Transubstantiation, the belief that in the Eucharist, the bread and wine are converted into the body and blood of Christ; this doctrine had been defined authoritatively at the Fourth Lateran Council in 1215. Regensburg demonstrated that by 1541 the Protestants had moved well beyond Catholic orthodoxy, though justification was still in theory an open issue. It had also become clear that the Protestants were unlikely to receive sympathetically any proposals for reunion in the future.

The Catholic Council which was summoned to Trent by Paul III, and first met in 1545, was not therefore intended to achieve reconciliation with the Protestants. As Pietro Bertano, the Bishop of Fano, said in 1547, 'if it will not help those already lost to the Church, it will at least help those still in danger of becoming lost' (Buschbell, 1916, p. 762). Its main aim was to secure Catholicism in areas, such as Italy, where Protestantism had not yet become well established. Its doctrinal purpose was plain: to clarify the Church's teaching on justification, and to declare on other matters where the Protestants had departed from Catholic orthodoxy as already determined. The agenda for the debates was in effect limited to beliefs disputed by the Protestants. In the words of Hubert Jedin, the Council had to 'distinguish Catholic doctrine from the teaching of the reformers' (Jedin, 1947, p. 179). But because no clear doctrinal decisions on these matters had been issued before 1545, there was little agreement among the prelates who gathered at Trent about which alternative teachings should be declared orthodox. The discussions at the Council therefore reveal some of the range and variety of Catholic thought in the later Middle Ages and the early sixteenth century.

Four major theological tendencies can be identified at Trent. The first, sometimes a little confusingly called

'Evangelism' by historians, was represented by a group known as the *spirituali*. They shared many of the Reformers' psychological and religious insights, and some may even have been influenced by Protestant books from northern Europe; but unlike Luther, they drew back from the consequences of their convictions for belief in the role of a visible Church. Their opinion was expressed most outspokenly at Trent by the Englishman Richard Pate, Bishop of Worcester, and the Italian, Tommaso Sanfelice, Bishop of La Cava. The second, rather less close to the Lutheran position, was represented by Girolamo Seripando, the leading figure of the tendency labelled 'Augustinian', though he too believed that human efforts to overcome sin are defective. A third group, which included the Franciscan theologian Cornelio Musso, Bishop of Bitonto, followed the teaching of the thirteenth- and early fourteenth-century philosopher Duns Scotus; they also argued that human effort has only a limited role in justification and sanctification. The fourth and most influential group, however, were the Thomists, followers of another thirteenth-century theologian, Thomas Aquinas; they were represented at Trent mainly by the Dominicans. They argued that individuals can prepare themselves for justification, and that good works thereafter are of value before God in themselves. The Council's final statements on these doctrinal problems deliberately avoided the specialist vocabulary of medieval theology but, as a result of the Thomist contribution, they committed the Church to the belief that the individual should co-operate with God in the process of justification and sanctification. The initiative belongs to man and God, and not, as in Luther's view, to God alone. Faith and works are both necessary, and both worthy of reward.

One reason why the Thomists' approach prevailed was its appeal to a number of the Italian bishops present, who dominated the early doctrinal sessions of the Council. Between 1545 and 1547, over two thirds of those entitled to vote at Trent were Italian. These bishops wanted to secure a doctrinal definition which could be readily taught to, and understood by, their flocks in Italy, where the Reformation teaching had already been well received; they were anxious to avoid any declaration which might seem to reduce the importance of human effort, for fear that a statement which devalued works would undermine the moral order. Their motives at Trent were pastoral, rather than intellectual.

In April 1546, the Council declared that Tradition – the uninterrupted teaching of the Church, from the first century to the present – and the Bible were of equal authority. Luther's teaching on revelation was therefore rejected. In June, the Council declared that the sacrament of Baptism remits Original Sin entirely, leaving us 'innocent, immaculate, pure...and beloved of God ...so that there is nothing whatever to retard [our] entrance into heaven' (Alberigo et al., 1962, p. 643). Concupiscence – which Trent defined as 'an incentive' to sin – is not of itself held against us. Luther's doctrine on Original Sin was therefore condemned, and the ground prepared for the decree on justification in January 1547, which emphasized the individual's ability to co-operate in God's work. Man can, and must, prepare himself for justification: 'while God touches the heart of man by the inspiration of the Holy Spirit, man does not effect absolutely nothing as he receives that inspiration' (p. 648). This preparation is followed by justification, 'whereby man, formerly unjust, becomes just; formerly an enemy, he becomes a friend' (p. 649). And works are needed after justification: 'no one ought to become complacent because of his faith alone' (p. 651). Divine grace and human effort must co-operate; faith and works must both contribute. This declaration finally completed

11

the separation of Protestants and Catholics from the shared theological inheritance of the Middle Ages, and created a new, Catholic doctrinal orthodoxy. The results of the Council's later debates, on the sacraments, Purgatory, prayers to saints, images and indulgences, issued between March 1547 and November 1563, merely confirmed the implications of these earlier decisions.

This lengthy examination of the discussions at Trent might lead us to suppose that all intellectual debate within the Church should have come to an end when the Council closed. But the prelates at Trent had left a great deal undecided. Their declarations had in fact been carefully phrased to avoid condemning anyone who had not previously adopted Protestant teaching; as a result, observed Hubert Jedin, 'in all doubtful cases previously professed theological opinions [might] continue to be held' (Jedin, 1961, p. 309). And the debates certainly did continue vigorously after 1563: the Catholic Church was not the intellectual wasteland suggested by contemporary critics such as John Milton. The usual routine of acrimonious academic argument was again taken up after the Council, for the most part without the risk of heresy. But there were also two controversies of major significance, in which the Catholicism which had emerged from the Council – normally called Tridentine Catholicism – was severely challenged: the first concerned Jansenism, the second natural science.

The title Jansenism is derived from the name of a seventeenth-century Bishop of Ypres in the Low Countries, Cornelius Jansen (1585–1638). Jansen spent the last ten years of his life composing a treatise entitled *Augustinus*, which was published at Louvain in 1640, two years after his death. But the debate had actually started before he was born. The Council had affirmed the role of both faith and works in order to exclude

12

Protestant theories on justification and sanctification; it had not, however, made any detailed declarations on how free will and grace were related. In 1567, the opinions of a Flemish university teacher called Michel Baius (1513–89) were condemned by the papacy; it was asserted that he had taught that man cannot by his own free will do good works without grace. Baius had actually attended the Council, and he maintained in his own defence that his writings did not in fact contradict the declarations of Trent. His theories were attacked again some twenty years later by a Spanish Jesuit, Luis de Molina (1535–1600), in his *Concordia liberi arbitrii cum gratiae donis* of 1588. Molina tried carefully to balance free will with grace by suggesting that God gives his grace only to those he knows in advance will choose freely to accept it. It was not at all clear how far either Baius or Molina had strayed from the teaching of Trent, so a special Congregation was established in Rome to discuss the problems further, without however reaching a conclusion, between 1597 and 1606. All this was well before the publication of the *Augustinus*; and some of those who became involved in the Jansenist controversy were already under suspicion before 1640. In 1633, for example, a heresy charge was directed against the nuns at the Parisian convent of Port-Royal, which was later a noted Jansenist centre.

The content of Jansen's teaching has always been a matter for dispute, and the *Augustinus* is not an easy book to read. At its core, however, it seems to reduce the role of human free will by arguing that God does not give his grace to everyone; it is God, therefore, who determines which individuals are to be given an opportunity to co-operate with him, and so experience justification. This theory obviously echoed the tendency in later medieval religion to give God the initiative in his relationship with man. It also seemed to encourage

13

a desire to withdraw from activity in the world in order to concentrate on contemplation: the spiritual director at Port-Royal, Jean Duvergier de Hauranne, the abbot of Saint-Cyran, believed that 'God has reduced all of religion to a simple and interior adoration in spirit and in truth' (Duvergier, 1962, p. 298). Many of those called 'Jansenists' did in fact retreat from the world, and they criticized churchmen such as the Cardinal de Richelieu who became involved with the grubby demands of government and diplomacy. This did not mean that they rejected the institution of the Church: on the contrary, they had a very elevated view of the importance of the sacraments. They insisted that only a contrition based on repentance, and not a fear of punishment, was of worth in the confessional; and they were hostile to the practice of frequent communion, because they believed that each occasion required extensive and careful preparation. Their standards of morality matched these uncompromising devotional demands. They saw themselves as a spiritual elite, and condemned their opponents who they regarded as an unregenerate rump: Saint-Cyran affirmed that 'even among Christians, only a very small number are saved after death' (Sedgwick, 1977, p. 196). Not surprisingly, perhaps, Jansenism tended to appeal, at least in the seventeenth century, to those who could afford to separate themselves from the world, and so avoid the risk of compromising their standards with the imperatives of life in society.

A similar emphasis on God's initiative and the need for withdrawal from the world can also be traced in the writings of Catholic mystics. The *Ascent of Mount Carmel* written between 1578 and 1584 by the Spanish Carmelite John of the Cross (1542–1591), came under suspicion in 1618 for its teaching on the passivity of the human faculties; John's texts were again investigated in the late seventeenth and the eighteenth century on charges of

Quietism, a doctrine (condemned by Pope Innocent XI in 1687) which advocated a complete abandonment of the will to God as the way of perfection. At its most developed, this inclination to reduce the importance of human effort could lead to a refusal to undertake any activities in the world at all, to despise action as a distraction incompatible with the contemplative life. In the early seventeenth century, this desire to be rid of the world occasionally surfaced even among the Jesuits.

But such objectives were obviously impracticable for most Christians, who had a living to earn and families to support, and the tendencies we have examined among the Jansenists and the mystics had already been criticized by the Bishop of Geneva, François de Sales (1567–1622), long before the appearance of the *Augustinus*. In his *Introduction to the Devout Life*, first published in Lyon in 1608, François recognized the value of a life lived in the world: it would be ridiculous, he argued, for every husband to be as poor as a Capuchin, or for every craftsman to spend all day in church. 'It is an error, even a heresy, to wish to outlaw the devout life from the company of soldiers, from the workshop of artisans, from the Court of Princes, from the households of families' (François, 1609, p. 16). He developed the same theme in his *Treatise on the Love of God* a few years later: 'Devout hearts love not the love of God less when they are distracted in exterior necessities than when they pray. Their silence, their speech, their action, and their contemplation, their employments and their rests, do in themselves all equally sing the Hymn of their Love' (François, 1617, p. 727). A similar opinion shaped the thinking of the Jansenists' most persistent opponents, the supporters of the system of moral theology known as Probabilism, who tried to make religious development possible and appealing for the laity by not insisting always and only on the most uncompromising standards

15

of devotion and behaviour. They rejected the Jansenists' assumption that only the perfect life was acceptable to God: to insist on the ideal would, they feared, destroy the commitment and sap the moral effort of those whose circumstances made the contemplative life impossible.

Jansenism therefore formed part of a much wider debate within the Tridentine Church, and it was for this reason that it aroused such fierce controversy. The irony is that the Jansenists, who reduced the role of human effort in theory, required the highest standards of devotion and behaviour in practice; while their opponents, who maximized effort in theory, were prepared to compromise their standards in practice. In one sense, the controversy was really an argument about the nature of God: is he a God of Justice, or a God of Mercy? And is the Church consequently a club for the elite, or a society for all?

The century following the Council of Trent was a period of extraordinary intellectual vitality in Europe: the age of Bacon, Bodin, Cardan, Cervantes, Comenius, Descartes, Hobbes, Marlowe, Montaigne, Pascal, Rembrandt and Shakespeare. Christian orthodoxy was repeatedly challenged by new ideas from outside theology altogether. The most celebrated example of this ideological competition is probably the controversy over Copernican astronomy. Nicolas Copernicus (1473–1543) had outlined his theory that the sun, not the earth, was the centre of the planetary system in his *De revolutionibus orbium coelestium*, published in 1543. The Lutherans had immediately condemned it, but the Catholic authorities had issued no formal statement before Galileo Galilei (1564–1642) published his *Sidereus Nuncius* in 1610. In this book, and in his *Letters on the Sun Spots* of 1613, Galileo claimed to have demonstrated by observation the truth of the Copernican theory. A number of other astronomers had already adopted Copernicus' ideas by then: in 1596, for example, the German Protestant Johann Kepler claimed in his *Mysterium Cosmographicum* that he had proved what Copernicus had suggested by mathematical calculation.

The Church would probably have been prepared to tolerate the views of Copernicus as a hypothesis, but not as a statement of fact, for, as Cardinal Roberto Bellarmino (1542–1621) explained in 1615, 'to affirm that the Sun is, in truth, at the centre of the Universe ...is a very dangerous thing' calculated 'to injure the holy faith by suggesting that the Scriptures are false' (Galilei, 1934, p. 171). The Bible seemed to assume that the sun revolves around the earth: to deny the accuracy of the Scriptures on this one matter was, because it was interpreted literally, to impugn the reliability of its authors, and so to cast doubt on all their work. Galileo had tried to meet this argument in 1613 by suggesting that some of the language used in the Bible was figurative. But this theory – that 'some passages in the Holy Scripture are not strictly true' (Pagano and Luciani, 1984, p. 69) as Nicolo Lorini, one of Galileo's opponents, summarized it – allowed the individual to choose what to believe in the Bible. The Council of Trent had explicitly prohibited the use of private judgement in the interpretation of the Scriptures in 1546; Galileo's ideas therefore seemed to challenge Tridentine orthodoxy.

In the long run, of course, the Church had to accommodate the new science to its old doctrinal framework; but in the early seventeenth century, the controversy over Galileo's ideas forced the authorities into a hasty decision, provoked not so much by his science as by their fear of its pastoral consequences. Galileo was in the end condemned not for the content of his theories, but for disobeying an order not to teach them.

The evidence against him went much further than this, however, for Galileo was also accused of atheism. Natural science and atheism were often associated in the minds of contemporaries: Galileo's friend Paolo Sarpi (1552–1623), who was interested in anatomy as well as astronomy and mathematics, was accused of the same offence in 1607. The charge against Galileo was almost certainly untrue; the charge against Sarpi may well have been accurate. Certainly the thinking behind Sarpi's *Pensieri filosofici*, which were drafted, it seems, between the later 1570s and the 1590s, challenges some of the basic assumptions of the Christian tradition.

Catholics had always supposed that God intervened directly in the material universe to influence human affairs. Such a faith is, after all, fundamental to a religion which proclaims its belief in miracles and the Incarnation. Natural events were therefore interpreted as an expression of God's will. In 1577, during a sermon at S. Petronio in Bologna, Francesco Panigarola (later Bishop of Asti) insisted that, while it was possible to explain by natural causes the plague which had recently devastated many north Italian cities – 'how could there not be a plague in Venice with all those filthy and putrid canals?' – the disease was nevertheless a punishment from God: 'God brings about the purposes he intends here on earth by using natural causes – so we should not say that he is not responsible for them... earthquakes, seditions, and plagues, even though they are produced by natural causes, are nonetheless the scourge of God' (Panigarola, 1592, ff. 284v–285r).

Sarpi rejected this traditional subordination of the natural to the supernatural. For him, everything had only a natural cause: God had no role to play. A crucial influence on Sarpi's thought was the philosophy of

18

Pietro Pomponazzi (1464–1525), who had separated the natural from the supernatural so distinctly that he refused to accept that the human mind can by its own power apprehend anything at all about the claims of religion. Yet if everything can be explained without recourse to the supernatural, there is no need to accept the traditional teaching on miracles and the Incarnation; if natural events have natural causes, religious belief might well be dispensed with altogether. Christians who accepted the conclusions of the natural scientists could therefore find themselves drawn towards atheism. The Catholic authorities had good reason, perhaps, for their instinctive wariness of the challenge from natural science.

2 The Clergy and the Bishop of Rome

We have concentrated so far on the history of Catholic doctrine in the sixteenth and seventeenth centuries. But it was the full-time officials of the Church, the clergy, who were responsible for ensuring that those authorized beliefs made an impact on the world. So we must now turn to examine the quality and preparation of the bishops (including the Pope, who was Bishop of Rome); the secular clergy, who were normally responsible for the parish system; and the religious, or regulars, the men and women who followed a rule of life (in Latin, *regula*) – the monks, nuns, friars and members of the 'new orders' of the Counter-Reformation.

It is easy to criticize the late medieval clergy, and to suggest that they were responsible for the decline of spirituality and morality which the Protestant Reformers attacked so vigorously in the sixteenth century. From top to bottom, it was argued, the Catholic priesthood was corrupt and uncommitted. The papacy itself can hardly be excluded from these censures. There were occasionally popes whose lives and devotion were blameless, but most fell far short of the standards set by Nicholas V (1447–55) or Hadrian VI (1522–3). The notorious Alexander VI, Pope from 1492 to 1503, is best known, perhaps, for his devotion to his many children; Julius II, who was elected in 1503, seems to have been more comfortable on his horse than his knees; and Leo X, who succeeded Julius and reigned until 1521, had been a cardinal since the age of fourteen.

There were plenty of examples of scandals among the episcopate, too. No Bishop of Cremona, for example, managed to reside in his diocese between 1475 and 1560. The Spanish bishops were particularly celebrated for their involvement in worldly affairs. Antonio de Acuña, Bishop of Zamora from 1507 to 1527, led an army of 300 clergy during the Comunero rebellion in 1520, and later murdered his gaoler. But there were competent and pious bishops as well. One example is Gian Matteo Giberti, appointed Bishop of Verona in 1524, who made strenuous efforts to establish a disciplined pastoral administration in his diocese well before the Council of Trent.

We find a similar mixture of deficiency and commitment when we consider the secular clergy before the Council. Modern research certainly supports some of the Protestants' criticisms. Many clergy were non-resident: in the diocese of Sens, in France, up to 60 per cent of those responsible for a parish were absent in 1495. Many absentee priests entrusted their flocks to part-time substitutes, priests without fixed posts who wandered from place to place in search of work; their standards were often low, and they rarely seemed able to build up any sense of responsibility for the people entrusted to their care. Many clergy were poorly trained; many led wholly inappropriate life-styles. There were complaints at the time about clerics who lived with women; in some areas, as many as one third of the secular priests may have been guilty of concubinage. There were also stories of drunkards, gamblers, even of criminal priests, of clergy with no knowledge of doctrine

21

who were unable even to administer the sacraments. Naturally, these inadequate priests appear more frequently in the records than their conscientious colleagues, and it is important not to assume from a few examples that the medieval parish system was controlled by the corrupt. It is also worth remembering that the laity may not have expected the same sort of behaviour from their clergy that the Reformers did. Medieval priests were seen as part of the local community – often they came from the area where they worked – and as long as they performed their liturgical duties, their congregations normally made no complaint.

The religious orders before the Counter-Reformation were not wholly corrupt either. There were several reform initiatives among the established religious orders in the later Middle Ages and early sixteenth century. A number of reformed Benedictine Congregations were founded in the fifteenth century: one at S. Giustina, Padua, in 1412; the Camaldolese were reformed by the Venetian Paolo Giustiniani in 1520; a reformed order of Franciscans was recognized in 1517; and the Capuchins, another branch of the Franciscans, grew up around Matteo da Bascio from 1523. There were even some austere new orders created in the fifteenth century: the Minims, for example, who eat no meat, fish, or dairy products, were founded in 1435. These developments within the traditional forms of religious order have persuaded many historians that the Catholic Reformation has its roots in the period well before the Protestant Reformation.

But such reforms were occasional, and hardly sufficient to protect the Church from criticism and schism. A thorough reform of the clergy 'in head and members' was therefore still required in the sixteenth century: as Cardinal Reginald Pole argued in 1546, 'we ourselves are largely responsible for the misfortune that has occurred – for the rise of heresy, and the collapse of Christian morality – because we have failed to cultivate the field that was entrusted to us. We are like salt that has lost its savour. Unless we do penance, God will not speak to us' (Jedin, 1961, p. 26). The Council of Trent in January 1547 accordingly announced its great desire 'to apply itself to restore ecclesiastical discipline, which has entirely collapsed, and to amend the depraved conduct of the clergy and Christian people' (Alberigo et al., 1962, p. 657). Doctrine and reform were therefore discussed in parallel at Trent, and by 1563 the Council's rulings had established a new framework for the activities of the Catholic clergy.

The administrative reforms of Trent were carefully drafted to avoid any threat to the position of the papacy. The Council made no attempt to reform the Pope's own administrative machine in Rome, the Curia, and in their closing session the prelates stated that nothing they had decided previously should be taken as an attack on the Pope's authority. Earlier decrees had guaranteed the papacy's superiority over the episcopate by recognizing its right to appoint to all bishoprics in the Church. Naturally, the Pope might consult other authorities before selecting a candidate for a diocese, but it was emphasized that, 'in the ordination of bishops... neither the consent, nor vocation, nor authority... of any civil magistrate whatsoever, is required' (p. 719): governments, in particular, need not be involved.

This did not mean, however, that the Council wanted to diminish the bishops' power in their dioceses. It was made abundantly clear that a bishop's authority was 'above that of other inferior priests' (p. 684), and that an effective episcopate was an essential precondition for the restoration of a reformed administration and purified spiritual life in the Church. The Council therefore insisted on certain minimum qualifications before a man could be consecrated as a bishop. He had to be of legitimate birth, 'of mature age, and endowed with gravity of conduct and skill in letters' (p. 663); he must have been ordained at least six months before his consecration; and he should normally hold an academic degree in theology or law. Once appointed, he had to reside in his diocese: he could not do his duty, said the Council, if 'he abandons the flock committed to him' (p. 658). He could not accept any other beneficed position in the Church while retaining his bishopric, nor might he hold any government office. His 'principal duty' in his diocese was to preach, and to administer the sacraments; he had also to supervise and, if necessary, correct his clergy. The bishop made the final decision on the appointment of every parish priest in his diocese, and he was required to visit each parish at least once every two years to ensure that his clergy were performing their duties conscientiously. No clerics were exempt from his authority: any priest found living 'shamefully and scandalously' was to be removed from his post. Finally, bishops were to establish a seminary in every diocese for training new priests, and hold a synod of all their clergy once a year, where the problems of the diocese could be discussed and resolved. Some of these measures – the order to hold a regular synod, for example – were not new; others – such as the creation of seminaries – were innovations. But they were all intended to deal with the sort of abuse which, it was believed, had fostered and encouraged Protestantism.

Trent therefore set the Pope above the bishops, and the bishops above the clergy. This clear, hierarchical perception of the Church was carried down to the secular clergy, too, who were thought to be elevated by virtue of their ordination above the laity:

24

There is nothing which continuously instructs others unto piety, and reverence for God, more than the life and example of those who have dedicated themselves to the divine ministry. For as they are seen to be raised to a position above the things of this world, others fix their eyes upon them as upon a mirror, and derive from them what they are able to imitate. (p. 713)

It was therefore essential that the secular clergy, too, should be of the highest quality. All priests were required by Trent to have served with a good record for at least a year as deacons before their ordination, and all those presented for a benefice had to be able to pass an examination by the bishop. No man was to be ordained unless there was a post with an income in the diocese for him to fill. Parish priests were to reside in the area to which they were assigned, and no priest without an established post was allowed to work in a diocese. The priests' main responsibility was to preach, at least once every Sunday and every feast day; they must teach doctrine and morality, the sacraments and the customs of the Church, to both young and old in their parishes. They were to set an example to their flocks by the purity and dignity of their lives; even their clothes were to be markedly different, so that 'by the decency of their outward apparel they may show forth the inward correctness of their morals' (p. 692).

Priests who failed in any of these obligations were to be punished by their bishops – by dismissal if necessary; and the Council extended episcopal authority over aspects of the lives of the religious orders as well. When necessary, Trent insisted, the bishop did have the right to override the authority of the regulars' own superiors: he had to punish any regular who left a monastery or nunnery illicitly, reprove any individual who behaved scandalously, and correct any religious house where observance of the Rule had become irregular.

These Tridentine proposals for the reform of the clergy were matched by a vigorous papal programme for reform in the Roman Curia. After the election of Paul III in 1534 the nature of the papal administration was dramatically changed. Paul fostered reform whenever possible; and his successors – notably Paul IV (1555–9), Pius V (1566–72), and Sixtus V (1585–90) – were energetic reformers, with a reputation for doctrinal and moral probity, and a history of involvement in the work of the Church before their election. The problems faced by these Counter-Reformation popes in their attempts to reform their administration were, however, immense. Common practices included the sale of office and the issue of dispensations from Church regulations in return for cash. The need for a reform of the Curia had long been recognized: if such abuses could be eliminated, the Protestants' case against the Church would be fatally weakened. But there was, perhaps inevitably, opposition to change from within the Curia: it was argued that to make changes in response to criticism would weaken Rome's case by seeming to concede the Protestants' main arguments.

Early programmes for Curial reform were therefore only partially successful. Paul III encouraged the work of committed reformers like Contarini, Pole, Giberti, Marcello Cervini and Giampietro Caraffa. At the start of his reign, he established a special committee of cardinals to examine and supervise the Curia; in 1536, he convened another committee, which submitted a remarkable report in March 1537. This document, the *Consilium de emendanda ecclesia*, listed the most serious abuses in the Church (for which it recommended a restored episcopate as the most effective remedy), including those in Rome itself. More specialized committees were subsequently established to examine the reform of individual departments in the Curia. Paul III certainly changed the atmosphere in Rome, and identified the targets for reform in the future; but real change was still being obstructed by its opponents when he died in 1549.

As long as the Council was in session, Curial reform was necessarily delayed. Pius IV formally approved the Council's decrees in January 1564; in July, he issued a Bull requiring the whole Church to put them into effect. By the close of his reign, in 1565, the Tridentine and the papal Reformations had converged, and after the election of his successor, Pius V, reform 'in head and members' could become a reality. The most public effect of this reform in the Curia was the establishment of new executive departments called 'Congregations' to supervize the Church's administration. The most important were perhaps the Congregation of the Holy Office, founded in 1542 and reorganized by Pius V, which was responsible for protecting the Church's doctrine; the Congregation of Rites, founded in 1588 to oversee the implementation of Trent's decisions on the liturgy, and the cult of saints; and the Congregation for the Propagation of the Faith, founded in 1622 to supervise missions. Each Congregation was run by a group of cardinals, who reported directly to the Pope. By the early seventeenth century the Church's central administration was therefore better organized and much more closely controlled than ever before.

The Tridentine reform in the dioceses and parishes was more problematical. The Pope was master in his own city, unhindered by outside influences; the bishops and clergy had less control over their decisions. But there were bishops who carried out the provisions of Trent conscientiously. Throughout the Counter-Reformation the model of a reformed bishop was usually taken to be Charles Borromeo, Archbishop of Milan from 1560 to 1584. He was of noble birth, and very well connected – Pius IV was his uncle – but he had had a thorough education in the law, and exercised a beneficial influence in Rome, where he was the Pope's Secretary of State. From the mid–1560s he committed himself to the task of diocesan reform, and his dedication to his flock was demonstrated by his heroic work in Milan during the ruinous plague of 1576. A model national hierarchy was established in Ireland from 1618: by 1648, there were twenty-seven bishops in the island; they had all been educated at the best seminaries, colleges and universities on the European continent, and all of them resided in their dioceses where they created a new and effective ecclesiastical administration. Other countries, too, produced conscientious bishops, who eliminated abuse and made a lasting personal and institutional impact on the local Church.

But not all bishops were like Borromeo and the Irish. The archbishopric of Paris was held by four successive members of the Gondi family between 1569 and 1662. It was certainly an illustrious line, but its members were not always very assiduous in their diocesan duties. Jean François Paul de Gondi, usually known as the Cardinal de Retz, and the fourth in the sequence, was more interested in politics than the Church. He took a prominent part in the Fronde, against Cardinal Mazarin, in 1648–9, and was actually in prison when he succeeded his uncle, Archbishop Jean François, in 1654. He escaped from gaol a few months later, and spent the next seven years abroad. He returned to Paris in 1661, and then swopped his diocese for the wealthy abbey of St Denis. This willingness to view a bishopric as almost a piece of private property had clearly not been eliminated by the Council. In Venice, members of some of the dominant patrician families – the Corner, the Grimani, the Pisani – continued to pass on the more valuable dioceses of the city's mainland empire from one relative to another after the Council of Trent, just as they had done before.

Only a minority of bishops in the sixteenth and seventeenth centuries could be accurately described as zealous reformers. In France, for example, there were 108 bishops in office in 1614, of whom many had other jobs as well as their bishoprics: at least forty had other ecclesiastical posts, and thirty-eight held offices in the royal government; only forty-one had a degree in theology or law; thirteen or more were aged under twenty-seven at the date of their appointment; a quarter had not been ordained; and only thirty-eight held a diocesan synod.

It is clear, therefore, that even after fifty years the directives of the Council were still not strictly observed. But it would be wrong to assume that bishops who were obviously not committed reformers were all necessarily scandalously corrupt or incompetent: the explanation is normally more prosaic. Few bishops were able to establish a complete authority in their dioceses, despite the decrees of Trent. They did not always control all nominations to parishes: private patrons were still entitled after Trent to present their own candidates to many benefices, and a bishop could at best only delay the appointment of unsuitable individuals. In some areas, such as Naples, the papacy itself retained rights of nomination. Religious orders could still claim and exercise exemptions from episcopal authority, and bishops frequently complained that the papacy had issued new exemptions to their parish clergy, or overturned diocesan orders in the Roman courts.

Bishops also had to take account of the wishes and interests of their secular governments. The State

29

authorities were bound to be concerned with local ecclesiastical developments: Catholic rulers were naturally keen to secure a degree of religious uniformity in their territories, but they were not always happy to see the Church increase its area of competence, or even, perhaps, its efficiency of operation. A number of governments therefore extracted concessions from the papacy which enabled them to control Church appointments and finances. After signing the Concordat of Bologna with the Pope in 1516, the French Crown acquired the right to nominate its own bishops. An even more extreme example of state control was Spain. In 1508, Pope Julius II gave the Spanish Crown the famous *patronato real*, the right to present to all ecclesiastical benefices in the New World; and in 1523, Rome confirmed Charles V's right to nominate all prelates in Spain. The Spanish government was also able, over the years, to gather many ecclesiastical revenues into its own hands: it administered all Church income in the New World; it retained one third of all tithes in Castile; and it collected in Spain, Sicily, Sardinia and America the tax originally intended to raise money for the Crusade. The clergy in Spain and its empire were often seen by contemporaries as no more than Crown officials, and no reform could take place in the Church if the government did not first approve.

Despite the difficulties faced by the episcopal reform, there is evidence to suggest that the quality of the parish clergy in some areas did begin to improve. Certainly more of them than before were resident. By 1672–3, only six curés out of 138 were recorded as absent in the archdeaconry of Paris. In many areas the proportion of beneficed clergy who had received a seminary or university education increased, and priests were often more secure financially as well. Some figures suggest that clerical immorality had been reduced: in parts of

Brittany, for example, concubinage had been a problem in more than 35 per cent of parishes in 1554, but it was discovered in fewer than 3 per cent in 1665. Trent's ambition to emphasize the separate status of the clergy was also echoed in many diocesan regulations: in 1658, the statutes of La Rochelle insisted that 'the clerics of our diocese must often reflect that they have been raised to an estate that is so sublime and so holy' (Pérouas, 1966, pp. 34–5), and this distinction between clergy and laity was reinforced when bishops required priests to wear their cassocks at all times. The diocese of Vannes tried to break its clergy's local links with family and friends in the seventeenth century by ordering that no priest was to be given a benefice in his home area. Better educated than their flocks, and living a conspicuously more moral and less insecure life-style, a growing number of priests could now serve the laity without the encumbrance of any deep involvement in community affairs.

But these parochial reforms were not easy to sustain. The secular clergy were not always distributed evenly: in parts of the diocese of Léon in Brittany during the seventeenth century, there was one priest for every hundred or so inhabitants, while in parts of Lorraine there was only one for five hundred. And many parish priests still refused to reside. In 1649, for example, it was said that the parish priest of Bondy 'was never in the . . . parish, but resided mostly in Paris and elsewhere' (Delumeau, 1977, p. 184). Some parishes were therefore inevitably short of pastors, and many were still served by temporary or part-time priests, despite the provisions of Trent. The laity of Bourgneuf in Brittany reported in 1659 that 'now and then strange priests visit the parish, and then go away – some are here for a month, others for a week . . . without any real commitment' (Croix, 1981, pp. 1155–6). In some areas, the devotional life of the

31

Church stopped altogether: the inhabitants of Changé in Anjou complained in 1645 of 'the abandonment of all regular services in their church' (Avenel, 1886, p. 335). Many priests were still very poorly trained: in 1617, Vincent de Paul came across a priest in Picardy who did not even know the words of absolution. And episcopal visitations continued to uncover immoral and scandalous clergy in the seventeenth century. Bishop Domingo Pimentel's visitation of the 400 seculars of Córdoba in 1638 discovered fifty-seven who were not living in chastity, forty who used their property to sell wine, twelve who ran gaming houses, eight who carried weapons, and six who were reported to be usurers. There is evidence too of negligent and uncommitted priests. In 1639, the dean of Saint-Germain-l'Auxerrois had to issue an order to prohibit his canons from 'taking their dogs with them into the choir, and sleeping, swopping places, gossiping, or reading books during services' (Avenel, 1886, p. 332). As late as the mid-seventeenth century, a cleric in Anjou reported that he had visited areas where parishioners told him 'that not once had they made their confession to their parish priests and confessors' (Abelly, 1664, p. 2).

These contrasts in the implementation of parochial reform are worth emphasizing. To a certain extent, they reflect the imperfect development of seminary training in the Church. The higher intellectual and moral standards of the secular clergy can often be linked with the creation and expansion of seminaries; but a seminary training by itself was no guarantee of improvement. Few seminaries actually provided a full training in the Scriptures, or in doctrinal theology; some bishops clearly thought that an academic background of this kind was not essential for a parish priest, who would spend most of his career among an illiterate, and often rural, population. Carlo Bascapé, the reforming Bishop of

Novara from 1593 to 1615, actually warned his clergy to avoid complex doctrinal problems which the laity would simply find confusing. This was a practical, not an intellectual, approach to Christianity; but it is not surprising, in the circumstances, if a few even of the seminary-trained clergy slipped away from doctrinal or moral probity after ordination.

In some areas, however, the diocesan seminaries were increasingly influenced in the seventeenth century by more rigorous clergy, such as the Jansenists, who produced ordinands in their own image. Support for their doctrinal and moral severity therefore increased among the parish priests of these areas: it has been estimated, for example, that thirty-eight of the sixty-eight curés in the city of Paris between 1653 and 1662 were at least sympathetic to the Jansenists; only nine seem to have been consistently hostile to their policies. Many bishops were evidently disturbed by this infiltration, and their suspicions were often encouraged by the adoption by many parish priests of the theories of Edmond Richer, whose *De ecclesiastica et politica potestate* was first published in 1611. This complex little book contains the idea that, while the Pope holds the highest rank in the Church, ecclesiastical government has been entrusted to the whole clergy. In parts, the book reads like a restatement of medieval Conciliarism, the belief that supreme authority in the Church lies not with the Pope but with Councils representing the whole Church. The popularity of Richer's book terrified the bishops of France, who foresaw an ecclesiastical revolution in which their own position would be overthrown: Dominique Séguier, the Bishop of Meaux, believed in 1656 that the parish priests were preparing 'a plot and a usurpation of the authority of the bishops' (Golden, 1981, pp. 82–3).

But only the richer dioceses could afford a seminary: even in Italy, more than half of the 290 or so dioceses

33

had still not built one by 1630. Many, perhaps most, priests therefore took up their posts without any systematic intellectual training at all; as a result, in many areas the doctrine of the Council of Trent was not adequately taught, and the abuses of the later Middle Ages and early sixteenth century remained prevalent. In some respects, the success of Trent's campaign to build a newly self-conscious clerical caste in society created as many problems for the future as its failure. By restoring confidence to the parish priest, the Council may have unwittingly contributed to the distrust between the upper and lower clergy which developed in some parts of the Catholic world in the seventeenth century; and by separating the parish priest from his flock, intellectually, socially, and financially, the Church risked alienating the clergy from the laity as well. If priests continued to conform to the aspirations of lay society – as they had before the Council – the Catholicism of Trent would soon be distorted or forgotten; but if they refused to adapt the standards demanded by the Council, its directives might be ignored altogether.

The aspirations of Trent were reflected much less ambiguously in the history of the new religious orders of the Counter-Reformation, even though several of them actually predated the Council. The Theatines were founded in 1524, the Barnabites in 1530, the Somaschi in 1532, the Ursuline nuns in 1535; the Society of Jesus was approved in 1540; and the Italian Oratorians emerged in the mid-1560s. There were more foundations in the seventeenth century: the Visitandine nuns in 1610, the French Oratory in 1611, the Lazarists in 1625, the Sisters of Charity in 1633, the Society of Saint-Sulpice in 1642. There was some opposition to these 'New Orders' in their early years – even Ignatius Loyola (d. 1556), the founder of the Jesuits, had to explain himself on more than one occasion to the authorities; but no attempt was made to replace the established religious families, which continued to engender their own reformed congregations well after the Council of Trent. The Discalced Carmelites, for example, developed in the 1560s, and the Trappist reform of the Cistercian order was introduced in 1662.

The new orders, however, were inspired by very different motives, and they shared a number of characteristics which distinguished them markedly from the monastic and mendicant orders of the Middle Ages. They were usually founded for a precisely defined social purpose: the Camillians, for example, were established in 1584 to care for the sick, the Piarists in 1597 to give elementary education to poor children in the city. Such charitable work was not inspired merely by an awareness of the demand for care in the ugly social and economic conditions of the sixteenth and seventeenth centuries. Several reformers, including Philip Neri (1515–1595), the inspiration for the original Oratory, taught their followers 'to leave God for God' (Certeau, 1965, pp. 340–1; Ponnelle and Bordet, 1932, pp. 219–20) – to leave God in prayer at the altar, and find him in the dispossessed on the street. To care for the poor was an act of devotion, as well as an act of social utility. In the Counter-Reformation, charity and piety were complementary: works and grace had to co-operate in practice, as well as in the doctrinal theory of Trent.

But if they were to fulfil this mission, the new orders had to have an organization and structure that would enable their members to get out of the cloister and into the world. They therefore normally dispensed with the traditional regulations which enclosed the older orders within a monastery or convent. The Jesuits were even exempt from the obligation to recite the offices together. They still followed a Rule, of course, but their regime

35

was quite different from that of the monastics and mendicants. The new orders were, in fact, a properly Counter-Reformation development: they owed nothing to medieval tradition. At their best, they were an expression of the same active spirituality that triumphed at Trent: a Christianity which was engaged in the world; man's effort co-operating with God's grace.

3 The Laity and the New Catholicism

Our examination of Catholic doctrine and the clergy seems to demonstrate that a 'new Catholicism' emerged in the Counter-Reformation. Its origins obviously lie in the later Middle Ages; but it was the Council of Trent which guaranteed its triumph. Its most characteristic feature was its insistence that the individual can, and should, co-operate with God, and that the Christian faith is best lived in activity in the world. Trent thus redefined the limits of intellectual orthodoxy, and created the framework for a renewed priesthood. But once the Council had been closed, the clergy had to take its doctrine back to the laity.

Certainly, the laity needed instruction. 'There is the greatest ignorance among the people', wrote a bishop to Vincent de Paul in 1651: 'in truth, the greater part of those called Catholics are Catholics only in name, because their fathers were Catholics before them, and not because they know what it means to be a Catholic' (Abelly, 1664, p. 3). In many areas, indeed, the laity were apparently ignorant of the most basic elements of Christianity. One priest, after visiting a town just south of Rome in the seventeenth century, reported that 'the majority of the men and women do not even know the

Lord's Prayer or the Creed, let alone the other things necessary to salvation' (Abelly, 1664, p. 58).

But ignorance of authorized Christianity was not the same as lack of any religious belief. The religion of the laity – often called 'popular religion' – has only recently become the subject of detailed historical research. Some historians dislike the term 'popular religion': William Christian, for example, prefers to distinguish between 'religion as practised' by the laity, and 'religion as prescribed' by the Church. But 'popular religion' seems to be a serviceable enough label, as long as we remember that the beliefs it describes were not necessarily limited to a particular social or economic group, and might vary according to time and place. It is not always easy, however, to determine the exact beliefs of the laity in early modern Europe. The majority were illiterate, and could not record their convictions on paper; and if their faith was seriously inconsistent with Christianity as taught by the Church, they would be unlikely to provide reliable information about it to any literate observers, for fear of encouraging further official investigation, and possibly punishment. Yet the evidence that survives in the records of ecclesiastical visitations and judicial tribunals does give the historian some guidance, which can often be combined with contemporary reports of customs, festivals and rituals. What has been revealed by this kind of research is a pattern of belief and behaviour with its own intellectual coherence: not exactly an alternative to Christianity, but based on assumptions which ecclesiastical reformers did not share.

Men and women in early modern Europe lived frighteningly close to the limits of survival, threatened at all times by the risk of hunger and disease which they could not readily prevent or relieve. The chief purpose of their religious belief was therefore to secure protection from these disasters. Popular religion was primarily

38

functional, rather than devotional. An intriguing example of this is provided by the *benandanti* of Friuli, in north-east Italy, who have been studied by Carlo Ginzburg. The *benandanti* claimed that they regularly did battle with the enemies of the harvest to defend the fertility of the community's land. Related beliefs have been traced in other parts of Europe – sometimes in only a very attenuated form, in the guise of myths and fantasies about female deities with the power to bring the dead back to life and to turn shortage into prosperity. Ginzburg has argued that such beliefs were the remnants of an ancient agrarian cult, independent of Christianity, but by no means hostile to it. Whether or not the 'night battles' of the *benandanti* took place in reality, they clearly demonstrate the leading preoccupation of popular belief: to protect the material welfare of the community.

Such an approach to religion was not very concerned with theological doctrine, but it did have a clear moral dimension. It was interested in the well-being of the community: any act which threatened the community was therefore believed to be wrong. It did not, however, have a developed concept of sin, in the Christian sense of an act which was wrong yet did not necessarily harm anybody else. In popular religion, one's relations with neighbours were of more immediate importance than one's relations with God.

This use of religion was not incompatible with Christianity; but it was likely to receive the teachings of the Church in terms which were already understood by the religion as practised, rather than those intended by the religion as prescribed. Saints, for example, were welcomed not as models for Christian living – which is what the Church intended – but as communal representatives with powers to protect and heal. Within twenty-five years of his death in 1624, 173 cures had been attributed to the Capuchin, Honoré de Paris, who was popularly reputed to be a saint in the area around his tomb at Chaumont-en-Bassigny. Among the grateful beneficiaries was Françoise Durant: having received the last rites after falling ill with a fever, she recovered on swallowing a cooked plum in which had been placed a hair of the holy man's beard. Statues of the saints were seen not as memorials to aid devotion, but as objects to be used in rituals to demonstrate the community's anxiety. In parts of the kingdom of Navarre, for example, during periods of drought large crowds would accompany the statue of St Peter in procession and then plunge it into the river, to encourage the saint to bring rain. Local people maintained in the mid-sixteenth century that he had never failed to deliver a good downpour within twenty-four hours of the ceremony. Ecclesiastical rituals which seemed to honour such well attested saints, including pilgrimages and the formal decoration of their altars, were always well attended by the laity; but the authorized liturgy and spiritual life of the Church was only sparsely supported by comparison. Christophe Sauvageon, the parish priest of Sennely-en-Sologne, south of Orléans, between 1676 and 1710, complained of this negligence in his memoirs: his parishioners, he wrote 'are superstitious rather than devout. Who could deny this, seeing they are rigid observers of various practices and rites which are both deplorable and ridiculous, and which serve only to distance them from true piety?' (Bouchard, 1972, p. 341).

The medieval Church did little to reduce this distance between popular and authorized religion. Laymen born into a Christian family rarely, if ever, heard a sermon. Mendicant friars – members of the Franciscan and Dominican orders founded in 1209 and 1220–1 – certainly committed themselves to preaching, especially during Lent and Advent, when they might be invited

40

to give a series of sermons in a parish church; but they tended to restrict their main activities to towns, often to the neglect of rural areas. Elsewhere, and at other times of year, the laity received very little formal instruction in Christian doctrine. The villagers of Saint-Jean-de-Boisseau, near Nantes, complained in 1561 that they were 'very rarely visited by preachers'; and in 1564 the faithful at Fégreac maintained they heard only four or five sermons a year.

The Church of the Counter-Reformation, however, mounted a concerted campaign to eliminate popular religion and to persuade the laity to accept authorized Catholicism. The reformers realized that they would first have to improve the parishioners' knowledge of the Church's teaching. Although the Council had insisted that bishops and priests should preach more regularly, many bishops believed the task was too great for the parish clergy alone, so they summoned members of the new religious orders to preach as well. In 1619, for example, the Jesuit authorities at Amiens, in north-east France, agreed to a request 'to send every year two members of our Company for several months to catech-ize, confess and instruct the common people' (Deyon, 1967, p. 380). In the first half of the seventeenth century, the Jesuits were probably the most frequent missioners: Michel Le Nobletz, for instance, began his missions in Brittany in 1608. But other orders were also important. The Oratorian John Eudes was preaching in Normandy by the 1630s, and the Capuchins had been invited to the diocese of La Rochelle by the 1650s. One religious order, the Lazarists, was founded specifically to conduct such missions: Vincent de Paul, their founder, insisted that they 'should not leave a village until everybody has been instructed in the things necessary for salvation, and until each person has made a confession' (Chalumeau, 1958, p. 326). Some of these missioners were extraordinarily conscientious: the Jesuit Julien Maunoir preached no fewer than 439 missions between 1640 and 1683 – an average of about ten each year.

In the early seventeenth century these missions were still conducted on a relatively small scale, but from the 1650s they became both larger and more carefully organized. Maunoir's missions, for example, sometimes contained as many as fifty priests, each working a twelve hour day on duties assigned by the team leader. They stayed in an area or diocese for a month or so, following a timetable of activities agreed in advance. Maunoir's suggestions for lessons on doctrine are typical of his systematic technique: each one, he advised, should last for at least an hour; it should begin with prayers and the commandments, recited by the whole group of clergy and laity together, and continue with a test of what had been learnt in the previous lesson, before starting on new material. Instruction should be carefully structured, and based on simple formulas which could be memorized. Examinations were to be held regularly. Frequent repetition, he believed, helped the learners remember their lessons.

Unlike the medieval preachers, the missioners of the Counter-Reformation devoted much of their attention to rural areas. The Lazarists, in particular, were committed to the task of taking Christianity to what Vincent de Paul called 'the poor people in the fields' (Abelly, 1664, p. 3), but they were not alone. In 1613, for example, the Oratorians established a special fund to finance regular missions to the villages outside Paris. To increase the impact of their teaching in agricultural areas, many missioners adapted their message to the convenience and expectations of the local laity. They were careful, therefore, to avoid harvest and vintage, when agrarian workers would not be able to attend; and they often used visual aids to attract or hold the attention of the illiterate. Each mission would begin with a dramatic display of devotion: a great outdoor procession carrying an image or a crucifix, to the accompaniment of loud songs, attending the consecrated Host; perhaps then making a bonfire of profane pictures and elaborate clothes. Preachers in Italy often beat themselves in public, or dressed as characters from the Bible – as Christ himself, sometimes, with a crown of thorns. To fix their teaching in the minds of an unsophisticated audience, some missioners used naive paintings as a focus for their instruction, and the Jesuits often improvised theatrical performances with musical accompaniments to re-enact the stories from the Scriptures or the lives of the saints. Others adopted contemporary melodies for devotional purposes: in the early eighteenth century, for example, a new French 'Invocation to the Holy Spirit' was set to the tune of the well-known popular song 'I don't know if I'm drunk'.

But the most reliable methods of Christian instruction remained the sermon and the catechism – though even these had to be as simple as possible for the benefit of an untrained laity. Sermons, in the vernacular, had to be unambiguous and easily memorable; the doctrine had to be no more than elementary. The best known catechism of the sixteenth century was Peter Canisius's *Summa Doctrinae Christianae* of 1554, but a great many new ones were printed in the seventeenth century. Each volume included basic information about God, the Incarnation and the Redemption, and encouraged regular use of prayers and the sacraments; but they could not provide a complete training in Christian doctrine. It was recognized that conversion was a gradual process, and the complexities of doctrinal theology were therefore avoided in the catechisms. Many missioners also set aside the strictest requirements of Catholic morality in their pastoral work: the followers of John Eudes, for example, were said to be fierce in their sermons but 'mild as lambs' in the confessional.

This tendency to dilute the demands of Christianity was frowned on, however, by missioners who were sympathetic to the devotional and behavioural standards associated with the Jansenists. They were concerned more with the interior, spiritual life of the laity than with converting them to a new set of intellectual beliefs. In the catechism issued by the bishops of Angers, La Rochelle and Luçon in 1676, Christianity was presented as a 'life in the school of Christ'; they offered a contemplative, almost a mystical, approach to salvation, placing emphasis above all on the interior disposition of the soul and its union with Christ.

There were therefore two contrasting approaches to mission work among the Catholic laity in Europe; both contained an inherent risk of failure. The missioners sympathetic to the Jansenists dealt with a level of religious awareness which bore little obvious relation to life in the world; as a result, they tended to appeal only to a minority. Their opponents, who adapted their doctrine to the needs and conditions of the laity, were probably more popular; but when they simplified their teaching to make it more effective, they ran the risk of changing its essential nature, and so of distorting it.

To meet these dangers, it was essential to establish a reliable system of education and pastoral care after the missioners had moved away. Parish priests and members of religious orders therefore involved themselves in teaching children outside church services, in schools which provided them with an elementary education at the same time as an authorized religious training. The Ursulines, for example, an order of women dedicated to Christian education, were founded in 1535 by Angela Merici in northern Italy, and later spread throughout

Europe and America. Often, the clergy were supported or assisted by pious members of the laity as well. Another Italian initiative was the 'Schools of Christian Doctrine', established from 1536 by Castellino da Castello to teach reading and writing as well as religion; they were staffed by the laity, and met on Sundays and feast-days. By 1611 the city of Rome had seventy-eight such schools, with 10,000 pupils, boys and girls aged from five to fifteen or more, meeting in relatively small classes. Education of this kind was quite widespread by the seventeenth century, even in rural areas: in 1673, only sixteen of the 129 parishes in the archdeaconry of Brie had no school.

Reformers also encouraged the development of a more effective liturgical life in the parish as another way of diverting attention from the rituals of popular religion. They tried to increase the laity's awareness that the parish church was a sacred place by prohibiting its use for irregular local ceremonies. Bishops such as Charles Borromeo banned dancing and other local festivities on Sundays and holy days. Greater emphasis was placed on the correct and reverent reception of the sacraments. In many areas, taverns were closed and services rescheduled to ensure the people had no excuse for not attending Mass, or for leaving it early. New devotional practices were introduced, often with the same effects. The 'Forty Hours' Devotion', for example, in which the consecrated Host was exposed and a rota of the faithful organized to pray before it, seems to have originated in Italy in the sixteenth century; in time, it took on some of the trappings of a popular festival, with a grand opening procession accompanied by large crowds and special music. The laity were thus tempted into playing an active part in parish life, reminded of authorized doctrine (in this case, of Transubstantiation), and impressed with the sacredness of the sacrament at the altar.

Most parish activities, including catechism classes, church services and the Mass, were carried out in public. The sacrament of Confession, however, brought the lay person into direct, individual and repeated contact with a priest in private, and so provided the Church with an opportunity to educate the individual layman in Catholic doctrine on a regular basis. In the confessional, the clergy could supervise the gradual assimilation of 'religion as prescribed' in place of 'religion as practised'. The conscientious priest could also use it to investigate the moral life of his people, and to influence their behaviour by creating within them a productive sense of guilt which only the Church could then remove. Catholic reformers therefore made great efforts in the sixteenth century to increase the use of the confessional, and John Bossy has suggested that they may also have changed its emphasis: whereas in the Middle Ages Confession had served to guarantee social harmony in the community – a concern that mirrored the preoccupations of 'religion as practised' – the Counter-Reformation used it to develop the private discipline of the individual. If this is true, the confessional must have been one of the most significant of the Church's weapons in its war against popular religion.

Another traditional feature of Church life which was transformed by the Counter-Reformation was the confraternities. These lay associations, which had existed since at least the thirteenth century, were normally dedicated to a particular devotional practice, and selected their members from a predetermined group – those engaged in a common occupation, for example, or resident in the same area. In Lyon, there were sixty-eight or more such Catholic confraternities in the sixteenth century: the Confraternity of the Pilgrims of St James of Compostella was one of them, its membership restricted to retailers and shopkeepers. Membership of a group such as this was attractive because it provided a source of social, economic and emotional protection and security in anxious times. Many confraternities operated a welfare system for their members, offering insurance against unemployment or assistance with medical expenses, and guaranteeing them a decent funeral, prayers for their souls after death, and support for their bereaved families. In the Middle Ages, the existence of these lay brotherhoods sometimes encouraged a fragmentation of church life; many were committed to beliefs and practices more in line with popular religion than authorized Catholicism. But during the Counter-Reformation, the Church recognized their potential, and tried to bring them under closer clerical or episcopal supervision. Many new organizations were created by reformers in the sixteenth and seventeenth centuries, which were used to assist the parish clergy in their pastoral duties. Teachers at the Schools of Christian Doctrine, for example, were all members of a lay confraternity. They could also be used to encourage attendance at and reverence for church rituals: by the end of the sixteenth century, 556 of the 763 parishes in the diocese of Milan had a fraternity of the Blessed Sacrament to increase devotion to the Eucharist. The Church could also take advantage of the confraternities' disciplinary structures: members found guilty of misbehaviour – of blaspheming, for instance – could be fined, and even at times expelled. The confraternities therefore gave the clergy another mechanism for influencing lay attitudes to religion.

The Church also used the opportunities provided by organized systems of poor relief. The sixteenth and seventeenth centuries were a time of severe economic difficulty in Western Europe: there was a desperate need for regular and generous help for the large numbers of poor and unemployed, the homeless and the vagrants on the streets and highways – for handouts of food,

47

clothing and money, for cheap housing and free medical care. Provision of this kind was justified by the demand. But involvement in such public activity could also be interpreted as an act of private virtue, as a way of serving Christ in the poor; in addition, it afforded the clergy and the pious an opportunity to foster the spiritual welfare of the unfortunate and indigent, who might otherwise have had little or no understanding of authorized religion. In Lyon, for example, material relief was given only to those who knew their catechism. Here need, virtue and propaganda all converged.

A further way of attracting the laity was to adopt popular customs for use in the authorized religion. Calendrical celebrations like May Day or Midsummer were sometimes tolerated for ecclesiastical use after they had been stripped of their more obviously disagreeable elements, and the *Rituale Romanum* issued by Pope Paul V in 1614 included ceremonies for blessing houses, marriage beds, images, fruit trees and vines, as well as rituals to ask for rain or fair weather. But in many areas zealous reformers demonstrated a more rigorous determination to eliminate such practices, which they often labelled 'superstitious'. Vittore Soranzo, who was Bishop of Bergamo in north Italy between 1547 and 1557, prohibited his flock from drawing the 'water of San Narno' from a well at the church of S. Alessandro when he discovered that local priests claimed it could heal all diseases when drunk on certain days of the year.

The Inquisition was often used to reduce lay reliance on popular cults of this kind. Tribunals of the Inquisition had been established in the Middle Ages throughout southern, central and western Europe. The infamous Spanish Inquisition, however, was a later and a separate development, a national organization of twenty-one regional tribunals under a central *Suprema* which reported to the king. The first tribunal began work in 1481, the last in 1638. By 1700, they had probably handled nearly 200,000 cases. Before 1540 they were preoccupied with investigations against Jews, especially those who had been baptized and who, it was alleged, often retained their ancient Jewish beliefs and customs. After 1540, the Spanish tribunals shifted their attention to suspects of Christian descent. Their busiest period was between 1540 and the 1580s, but their activities decreased in the seventeenth century: they dealt with twice as many cases between 1540 and 1615 as between 1615 and 1700. The second half of the sixteenth century was also a busy time for the older Inquisition tribunals in Italy and France, and for the tribunals in Portugal (established in 1536) and in the Iberian colonies of America and Asia.

The Inquisition was directed to uproot all alternatives to orthodox Catholic teaching. Naturally, the tribunals investigated heretics, and supervised the content and distribution of books. But they also had authority to prosecute Catholics found guilty of moral offences: between 1560 and 1614, 50 per cent of the cases investigated by the Spanish Inquisition involved offences like bigamy, fornication, sodomy and blasphemy. The Inquisition can therefore be seen as yet another weapon in the Church's campaign to control belief and behaviour.

The clearest example of the Inquisition's assault on popular belief is probably its treatment of witchcraft. In many tribunals, the number of trials for magic and witchcraft increased in the Counter-Reformation; one calculation suggests that in Venice the proportion of such cases rose from about 12 per cent in the sixteenth century to nearly 50 per cent in the seventeenth century. It was commonly assumed that an individual brought down by impotence, illness, economic failure or death might be a victim of *maleficium* or sorcery employed by

49

an enemy, and charges of this kind frequently emerged out of the tensions of community life. Those accused were often isolated and unprotected, men as well as women; often they earned a living as healers, midwives or wetnurses. But sorcery was not normally associated in popular belief with night-flying, Sabbats, cats and sexual liaisons with the devil: these were elaborations produced by the intellectuals and theorists of the later Middle Ages. Obviously, there were links between the popular and the more educated approach to sorcery and witchcraft, and over time, no doubt, each one adopted components from the other for its own purposes. But in the sixteenth century it was the academic stereotype that was taken up by the inquisitors; and sometimes it was imposed by them on activities that were really no more than outcrops of popular religion. One of the best known instances of this process is, again, the story of the *benandanti* of Friuli, who confessed their adherence to their agrarian cult, and were sentenced by the Inquisition as witches. Popular religion was here interpreted as witchcraft, and individuals were punished for crimes they had not committed, and probably did not even understand.

It is important, however, not to exaggerate the role of the Inquisition in this campaign against popular religion: it was rarely the bloodthirsty, insensitive or tyrannical monster its detractors have claimed. Rates of conviction were low in most tribunals, and the punishments imposed often slight. Even in Spain, less than 2 per cent of Inquisition suspects were executed at the notorious, and relatively infrequent, *autos da fé*. In Italy, the Congregation of the Holy Office exercised a restraining influence on the provincial tribunals, especially when dealing with cases of magic and witchcraft. Its insistence on rigorous standards of evidence certainly discouraged many local inquisitors from convicting suspects on charges of witchcraft: how could they prove in law that an accused woman had flown to a Sabbat at night in the form of a cat?

Historians have often argued that secular governments also helped to limit the excesses of the Inquisition; and it is certainly true that no tribunal could operate or enforce its sentences without the support of the State. But during the Counter-Reformation Church and State were normally in agreement about the need to discipline the laity: neither believed in the advantages of freedom of thought or action. When inquisitors punished heresy, prohibited books, or investigated popular religion, they usually met with the ready approval of the magistrates. Many governments were also happy to reinforce the Church's efforts to increase lay respect for the sacred: the 1571 town statutes of the small Tuscan community of Casteldelpiano, for example, prescribed very severe penalties for anyone joking, fighting, doing business or dancing in Church, 'because people today have so little respect – they have no regard for holy places, and even less for God' (Imberciadori, 1959, p. 442). Blasphemy in church was therefore punished with a fine of double the amount for the same offence committed elsewhere. At the same time, many governments tried to increase their own influence over the moral and spiritual lives of their peoples. Bruce Lenman and Geoffrey Parker (1980) have suggested that early modern governments began to 'criminalize' sin, by extending their jurisdiction to include religious and moral offences which were previously rather more the preserve of the Church. Where secular courts had in the past been concerned – like the Church, and like popular religion – simply to maintain social harmony, they now enforced a much more moralistic model of behaviour. Private activities, which did no damage to the community, were brought within the pale of the law.

51

In these ways, the campaign of the Counter-Reformation to increase clerical influence over the laity was matched by the policy of the State to increase government control over its subjects. No form of non-conformity would now be safe from investigation.

4 Missions and the Non-Catholic World

The Reformation is certainly one of the more conspicuous events of the sixteenth century in European history; but the most significant development of the period in world history was surely the establishment of European influence overseas, in America, Africa and Asia. Both presented a challenge to the Church of the Counter-Reformation: in northern Europe it was faced with the task of converting hostile Protestants; in the wider world there were millions of pagans to convert. The scale of missions overseas had to be much greater, of course, and the substance of their teaching had to be different too – the Protestants had rejected Catholicism, while the pagans had never heard of it; yet the problems of missionary work in each area were surprisingly similar, and the solutions selected often the same.

After the Reformation, the Catholic Church was barely represented in some parts of Western Europe: in Scotland or Scandinavia, for instance, Catholicism could survive only in secret. But points of contact between Protestants and Catholics were more common than is sometimes realized. In France, the Protestant population was given legal recognition after the Edict of Nantes had been signed in 1598; in parts of central Europe, the final outcome of the religious division was still not settled in the later sixteenth century, and Protestants and Catholics lived beside each other, sometimes quite peacefully. Economic and social links often survived the Reformation, despite the boundaries erected by doctrine and administration.

Catholic missionary techniques had to take account of these circumstances. In France, where the Church was protected by the government, missionary campaigns could be mounted quite openly. Members of the religious orders would establish themselves in or near Protestant communities, and issue invitations for public debates on doctrine. In the autumn of 1586, the Capuchins in Amiens ran a mission in the cathedral, and in suburban monasteries and churches; there was a sermon every morning, and a simulated disputation every afternoon, in which one Capuchin would present Protestant objections to Catholic belief and another would answer them triumphantly. These controversialists had to be well trained in the Scriptures, in Protestant theology, and in methods of argument: the more plausibly they presented their case, the more likely they were to persuade any Protestants who might be listening.

A greater awareness of the realities of Protestant commitment, however, taught many Catholics that conversion was only rarely achieved by one good argument; a less unwieldy and less abrasive approach to proselytism was therefore developed. The German Jesuit Martin Becan identified four types of 'heretic' in his *Manuale Controversiarum* of 1624, and advised a different strategy for each: be distant with the stubborn, he said, courteous with the zealous, stern with the indifferent, and fraternal with the uncertain. Vincent de Paul recommended Becan's book to his missionaries, and told them that in his own efforts to convert heretics he had discovered that gentleness, humility and patience were

54

more effective than brilliance, debate and abuse. The Jesuits also realized the advantages of reducing social antagonisms between Protestants and Catholics. By 1615 they had opened 373 colleges to offer young boys a basic schooling in the classics and in doctrine, and sometimes a training in natural sciences as well. This education was so highly regarded that in areas of Germany where Protestantism and Catholicism were both permitted, the sons of Protestants were often enrolled alongside Jesuit novices.

Missionaries in wholly Protestant countries had to be more discreet. Rome's authority in Sweden had been repudiated by Gustavus Vasa in 1524; some fifty years later, a Norwegian Jesuit called Laurentius Nicolai 'Norvegus' entered Sweden secretly, and acquired a post at the new theological seminary for the Protestant Church of Sweden. At first, he lectured only on those aspects of the faith which were common to Protestants and Catholics. Then he tried to reduce his listeners' instinctive prejudice against Catholicism. He next selected the more sympathetic students for private tuition, and began to question some specifically Lutheran doctrines in public. By the Easter of 1577, he had persuaded thirty young men at the seminary to renounce Protestantism, and the following summer a number left Sweden for further training in Rome.

This tactic of disguising Catholicism in a hostile environment was often accompanied by a readiness to adapt its rules at the same time to make conversion appear more attractive. It was argued at the Council of Trent, for example, that if the laity of Bohemia and South Germany were permitted to receive communion in both kinds – in other words, to take both the bread and the wine, as the Protestants insisted, rather than the bread alone, as Catholic tradition required – many of those who had separated from Catholicism might be encouraged to revert to it; and Pius IV eventually agreed. Similarly, when Mary Tudor acceded to the throne in England, it was suggested, even in Rome, that if the Protestants who had acquired ecclesiastical property under Henry VIII and Edward VI were allowed to keep it, they might be more willing to submit to the Church on other matters. In practice, these well-meaning attempts to increase the appeal of Catholicism therefore often depended on its dilution.

In many areas, however, the effectiveness of Catholic missions to Protestants was reduced by bad organization and poor support. The campaign in Scandinavia was initially sustained only by the extraordinary daring of Norvegus and his few secret associates. Appeals to Rome from Catholics in Scotland were persistently ignored, even by the Society of Jesus: in 1623, according to one report, there were only four Jesuits in the whole country. The missions obviously could not survive for ever on such a small scale and with so little encouragement. In 1598, Clement VIII established a special Congregation of Cardinals to oversee mission work; and in 1622, Gregory XV created a new Congregation called the Sacred Congregation for the Propagation of the Faith (*Propaganda Fide*) to deal with all those areas – Protestant and pagan – where there was no established hierarchy of bishops. Between 1622 and 1649, Propaganda founded forty-six new missions; and in 1627, a special college was opened in Rome to train missionaries. A more closely co-ordinated strategy was also developed by the religious orders. Vincent de Paul supervised his missionaries carefully and maintained a regular correspondence with his priests, whether they were preaching to Catholics in France and Italy, to Protestants in Poland, to pagans in north Africa and Madagascar, or even to the highlanders and islanders of Scotland – where one missionary to Eigg and Canna reported in

1652, 'I have discovered thirty or forty persons aged seventy, eighty, a hundred or more who have never even received baptism' (Abelly, 1664, p. 203).

The development of a more systematic administration of missionary work was a welcome response to the massive increase in demand for missionaries abroad. European 'expansion' began with Columbus's voyages to the Caribbean in the 1490s; from the sixteenth century, Europeans travelled to central, south and north America, to the coasts of Africa south of the Sahara, to India, the East Indies and the Philippines, to Japan and the Chinese mainland. And where the explorers and settlers led, the clergy closely followed. The Augustinians, for example, were in Mexico by 1533 and Peru by 1550; they reached the Philippines in 1565, Goa in 1572, and China in 1575; they founded houses in the Congo and in Angola in 1578, and in Muscat in 1596. By 1623, they were even in Iraq.

In one sense, it can be argued that the Catholic Church was able to compensate by overseas acquisitions for its losses in Protestant Europe; but its extension to the non-Christian world forced it to confront, for the first time in many centuries, the intellectual challenge posed by civilizations which had developed without any knowledge of the Christian religion.

The early pioneers and missionaries tended to assume that all non-Europeans were necessarily inferior to themselves. Indigenous peoples therefore needed careful supervision and control. In 1677 Felipe Fernández de Pardo, who was to become Archbishop of Manila in 1680, argued that it was the Filipinos' 'evil customs, their vices, and their preconceived ideas which make it necessary to treat them as children even when they are forty, fifty or sixty years old' (Phelan, 1959, pp. 189–190). Some Europeans agreed that certain non-

57

European societies were more admirable than others: the usual hierarchy ranked China, Japan and some Indian cultures above those of America, and put the Africans at the bottom. But they were all placed a long way below the civilization of Western Europe. And these assumptions were reinforced by the missionaries' professional conviction that Christianity was the only true religion: other religions were the products of evil or ignorance. When the Jesuit Francis Xavier arrived in Japan in 1549, he wrote, 'this land is all full of idolatries and enemies of Christ' (Schurhammer, 1982, p. 91); and in an account of Malabar in south-west India, written in 1615, another Jesuit, the Portuguese Diogo Gonçalves, repeatedly called the Hindu deities 'demons' and local beliefs 'diabolic superstitions' (Gonçalves, 1955, pp. 68, 70, 71, 94).

A number of missionaries were, as a result of these considerations, profoundly pessimistic about the prospect of converting non-Europeans voluntarily; and their doubts were apparently confirmed by the opposition of some local peoples to missionary activities. During the violent, and explicitly anti-Christian, Mixtón War of 1541 in New Galicia (Mexico), monasteries and churches were burned, friars were mutilated and murdered, and converts 'debaptized' by having their heads washed. Conversion was obviously a dangerous undertaking: even in the eighteenth century, a hostile pagan shaman in Paraguay used poisoned potatoes to kill a Christian chief called Roy. Manuel Uriate, writing of the Mainaus mission in the same century, succinctly summarized the missionaries' reaction to this sort of opposition: 'These barbarous peoples do not listen to the voices of the Gospel preachers unless they have first heard the sound of gunpowder' (Boxer, 1978, p. 73).

It was therefore often believed that a missionary campaign could only succeed after every trace of the pre-Christian civilization had been forcibly obliterated. Conversion required a total rejection of the pagan past – not just an assent to Christian doctrine, but the adoption of a European life-style. All temples, sacred groves and 'idols' had to be destroyed, local ceremonies banned, native customs replaced. In Mexico, this process was virtually complete by 1540: the slate, it was thought, had been wiped clean, ready for the imposition of the new civilization imported from Europe.

Few missionaries knew very much about the cultures they had thus helped to suppress. Their knowledge of native languages was frequently patchy, and their understanding of indigenous beliefs and assumptions only limited. Not surprisingly, perhaps, their insensitivity to local feelings often alienated those they wished to convert. In Japan, for example, where crucifixion had traditionally been the sign of a shameful death, it was scarcely productive to emphasize its role in Christ's Passion among the ruling elite; yet the Franciscan missionaries flaunted their crucifixes, and a number of other equally inappropriate devotional symbols, thus limiting their own effectiveness. And the high-handed policies of Christian secular authorities often further antagonized native communities. When a Christian was killed at Faza, East Africa, in 1587, the Portuguese simply sailed in and sacked the town.

This stolid indifference to local opinion can be at least partly explained by the survival of traditional apocalyptic and millenarian beliefs into the sixteenth and seventeenth centuries. Jesus had instructed his disciples to go 'into all the world, and preach the gospel to every creature' (Mark 16:15); but he had also told them that 'this gospel of the kingdom shall be preached in all the world for a witness unto all nations; and then shall the end come' (Matthew 24:14). Many Christians therefore believed that the discovery of new lands to the west, south and east of Europe was the prelude to the end of the world: 'once the Gospel has been preached throughout the world, the Day of Judgement will come' wrote the lawyer Juan de Solórzano Pereira in his *Política Indiana* of 1648 (p. 29). The missionary had a duty to preach to as many pagans as he could as quickly as possible, regardless of the reaction he provoked. These convictions were particularly influential in the early sixteenth century in Mexico, and in the second half of the century in the frontier areas as Spanish rule drove north and south into America; it remained strong in Portuguese territories in the seventeenth century.

But another explanation for their insensitive dismissal of pagan culture may be the missionaries' acute shortage of manpower. Early mission campaigns were often entrusted to individuals, unsupervised and working alone, who had to cover vast distances and take responsibility for huge populations in scattered and isolated villages. They had no time for discriminating tactics or systematic pastoral care. In the Peruvian district of Cajamarca, for instance, there were only a handful of missionaries for more than 500 villages in 1548; on the Bisayan islands of the Philippines there were often fewer than thirty Jesuits for up to 70,000 inhabitants.

These factors all worked against any thorough or coherent missionary activity. The preparation provided for baptism was often wholly inadequate; many, perhaps most, converts had little understanding of the religion they were adopting. Some missionaries did try to teach the fundamentals of Christian doctrine, but few had the linguistic skills to deal with more complex concepts like the Trinity, and sermons which have survived from overseas missions suggest that the arguments used to encourage conversion were frequently rather disreputable anyway. In Mexico, for example, audiences were told that they had to accept the Christians' God because their own gods had failed them so signally during the recent Spanish war of conquest. This reasoning was actually quite effective; but it hardly amounted to preaching the Gospel.

Even after baptism, some missionaries were reluctant to educate converts any further in religion. In Mexico and the Philippines, local people were not encouraged to receive communion because it was believed they could not understand it. Diego de Bobadilla explained in 1640 that although the Filipinos 'readily received our religion ... their meagre intelligence does not permit them to sound the depths of its mysteries' (Blair and Robertson, 1905, p. 295). In Japan, on the other hand, the Portuguese Jesuit Francisco Cabral insisted in the 1570s that neophytes should not be given a full training in Christian theology because 'once they become expert theologians ... they would be readily prone to divide the Law of Christ into heresies as numerous as the sects which their ancestors had evolved from the false doctrine of Buddha' (Boxer, 1951, p. 86). Convinced of their converts' stupidity, or fearful of their intelligence, the missionaries simplified the content of their teaching; and very few were prepared to contemplate ordaining native priests. As late as 1954, no African had been ordained in Mozambique.

No European, of course, could fail to notice the stark contrast between the assumptions of Catholicism and those of many pagan societies. In Peru, no man would marry a woman without a trial sexual relationship first – 'nobody can make a good wife who has not previously been a concubine', the missionaries were told (Boxer, 1975, p. 108). The Peruvians' rituals of courtship, marriage and family life were consequently quite different from those of Europe, and it was difficult to persuade them of the advantages of Catholic marriage or of the disadvantages of premarital sex. In the Far East, the contrast was intellectual rather than social. The Buddhists who talked with Francis Xavier in Japan had no concept of an afterlife or of a personal Creator, two fundamental beliefs of Christianity; for them, nothing had either a beginning or an end.

A number of missionaries nonetheless found it difficult to accept the assumption that all non-Europeans were necessarily inferior or irredeemably incapable of accepting the most elevated doctrines of Christianity. Vasco de Quiroga, who became the first Bishop of Michoacán in 1536, praised the Indians of New Spain for their natural, simple virtues, and declared that they were ready to receive any doctrine the Church might want to teach them. Some missionaries even believed that pagan societies had already acquired an understanding of religion without the aid of the Christian revelation or the Scriptures: in 1696, a French Jesuit asserted that the Chinese 'had preserved for nearly 2,000 years the knowledge of God' (Le Comte, 1696, p. 136). As a result, a less rigid and less impatient missionary strategy began to emerge, alongside the more belligerent methods already examined.

Missionaries who adopted this alternative strategy recognized that conversion was a slow process. Jerome Lalemant, a Jesuit in North America, in 1642 calculated that 'to make a Christian out of a Barbarian is not the work of a day' (Thwaites, 1898, pp. 206–7): it needed careful planning and preparation. First, the missionaries had to learn how to speak to their audiences fluently. They compiled grammars and dictionaries of native languages, and published translations of prayers, sermons and devotional works. The first catechism in the Nahuatl language of Mexico was published in 1539; the first in Tamil in 1554; the first in Chinese characters in 1584; and the first in any African language in 1624.

They recognized the need to understand the pre-Christian beliefs of indigenous peoples, and the problems created by the wholesale destruction of pagan temples and idols. In his *De Procuranda Indorum Salute*, a handbook for missionaries written in 1577 and widely used in Spanish America, the influential Jesuit José de Acosta observed that 'it has always seemed to me that the effort to eliminate idolatry by force first, before the infidels have spontaneously welcomed the Gospel, serves rather to shut and lock the door on the Gospel than to open it, as has been claimed' (Acosta, 1954, p. 561). Pagans had a right to humane treatment, and their traditions should be tolerated if at all possible. 'If something is not offensive to God', wrote Francis Xavier in Japan, 'it seems preferable not to change it' (Schurhammer, 1982, p. 239). Converts should be allowed to retain all those customs that were not actively opposed to the Christian religion: habits of eating and drinking, dowry and inheritance conventions, funeral and burial practices. A Jesuit at the Huron village of Lorette in New France (Canada) explained in 1675: 'after removing from them all the superstitions which they had learned in paganism, we have left them the remainder, which serves but to maintain the mutual union which exists between them' (Thwaites, 1900, pp. 32–3).

This was a more patient and deliberate approach to preaching the Gospel. According to Acosta, 'our duty is to advance, one step at a time, educating the Indians in Christian customs and discipline, and silently removing the superstitious and sacrilegious rites and habits of rude savagery' (Acosta, 1954, p. 502). Missionaries were therefore sent out in teams, to settle in one place and gain acceptance by the community. Extensive programmes of schooling were devised for children; Christianity was presented to adults in ways they could assimilate with ease. In the Philippines, for example, the Commandments, the Creed, and Christian prayers were put into verse which could be sung to the traditional chants used at work. Many missionaries adopted the local life-style: they dressed in local clothes, and were careful to observe the prevailing social conventions and rules of etiquette. Alessandro Valignano made use of Japanese educational methods in the 1580s, and urged his Jesuit colleagues to behave in ways the Japanese would understand and respect. Matteo Ricci, living in China between 1583 and 1610, accepted the social rituals of Confucianism; he adapted the Christian liturgy to suit the local calendar, and left out those parts which might cause offence. Robert De Nobili followed a similar policy in India, and even worked within the Hindu caste system. Such compromises with non-Christian cultures were designed to help the missionaries make friends among the local population; only after that could they hope to persuade them to accept the Gospel.

There were dangers, however, in such an accommodating attitude. Catholic tradition was not too seriously threatened, perhaps, when the Sorbonne declared that for religious purposes the beaver was a fish, so that converts in Canada could have something to eat during Lent. But the readiness to defer in this way to local circumstances sometimes endangered more weighty matters of Catholic doctrine. In some areas, missionaries were prepared to overlook the Church's rules on monogamy, in order to encourage conversions. In others, they tried to take up pagan cults for Christian use. In Macao, on the south coast of China, the Buddhist devotion to Kwan-yin was replaced by the Catholic devotion to the Virgin Mary. Where Kwan-yin had been the patron of sailors, Mary became the 'Star of the Sea', and images of the Virgin were designed to resemble those of Kwan-yin. In their quest for more productive methods of evangelism, the missionaries sometimes reduced even the most distinctive portions of the Catholic message almost beyond recognition.

A telling example of this process is provided by the missionaries' attempts to translate the essential concepts of Christian doctrine, such as God, sin and the afterlife, into languages which had no words for them. Some simply adopted the nearest equivalent in the local language; but the native words inevitably conveyed quite inappropriate conceptual associations. In China, Matteo Ricci had to use the same words for 'God' as the Chinese used for 'Emperor', and his character for 'the Mass' was borrowed from Confucian ceremonies in honour of the dead. In Japan, Francis Xavier took words from the Buddhist vocabulary for his catechism in 1549–50; but he soon discovered that this had caused some misunderstandings, and from 1551 he preferred to use Latin words for theological concepts instead. In Mexico, Peru and the Philippines, missionaries similarly retained the Spanish terms. But this solution simply brought them back to the original problem.

Some missionaries in America believed that the only wholly satisfactory method of teaching Christianity was to segregate converts into special villages, where they could be trained at length in isolation from their native environment. These 'Reductions' (*reducciones*) were established at various times in Canada, Mexico, Brazil and Paraguay, sometimes with great success. But while the neophytes were in this way separated from their pagan backgrounds, they were also kept apart from the influence of European societies on the continent, and any later integration between the two cultures was thus made almost impossible.

The difficulty of bringing together Christian teaching and non-Christian society bedevilled both the missionary strategies we have examined. One strategy accepted that

65

an individual could learn of God by an act of free will, without revelation; a pagan could discover much of the truth by the use of reason alone. The Church should therefore preserve and build on what was good in native culture, and Catholicism should be taught without reference to its European setting. The other strategy emphasized the individual's need for revelation and grace; a pagan, by definition, had neither. Native culture could therefore contain nothing of permanent value, and it should be erased and replaced; Catholicism and European civilization were inseparable. Neither strategy was very satisfactory. The first required such a dilution of Christianity that its message might be distorted; the second required such a disruption of social life that its attractiveness might be dispelled.

This was not merely a problem of presentation. The missionaries overseas had to answer the same crucial questions as their colleagues who preached to the Protestants and Catholics in Europe – questions which recall the debate examined earlier between the Jansenists and their opponents about the relation of free will and grace. Could the Gospel be reconciled to society? And should the Church make concessions to the world?

5 The Impact of the Counter-Reformation

In the later Middle Ages, there was a tendency in the Christian Church to concentrate on religion as primarily a personal experience, to assume that God would take the initiative in his relationship with mankind, and to withdraw from human involvements. The same tendency emerged on occasion after the Reformation, in the teaching espoused by the Jansenists and by Catholic mystics. But they were decisively rejected by the Council of Trent, which emphasized instead its belief in the need for an active involvement in the work of God. The doctrinal decisions of Trent were matched in the Counter-Reformation by the aspirations of the new religious orders.

But it is important not to separate Tridentine Catholicism too cleanly from its medieval roots, for it continued to share with many Christians of the later Middle Ages a preoccupation with the fate of the individual. The same concern, of course, can be traced in the theology of the Protestant Churches. Both focused their attention on the individual relationship between man and God, and urged the faithful to dedicate themselves in this life to securing the next, even though the Protestants taught the submission of the mind and will in faith where the

Catholics taught the exertion of the mind and will in effort. The most representative manifestation of these preoccupations in the Counter-Reformation is probably the confessional. The practice of confession is based on the belief that the difference between right and wrong can be grasped by the mind, and that we can choose to do what is right by an act of free will. During the sixteenth and seventeenth centuries, the confessional was used by the clergy of the Counter-Reformation to direct the laity's belief and behaviour, and it therefore reflected both the Tridentine insistence on co-operation with God and the later medieval stress on the individual.

The confessional was also used in the Counter-Reformation to detach the laity from 'popular religion', and here too we find that the aspirations of the Protestant and Catholic Reformations were at one. Popular religion tried to subordinate the spiritual world to the interests of the material world; the reformers, Protestant and Catholic, wanted instead to subordinate the material world to the spiritual. They therefore committed themselves to an assault on popular religion, and they were supported in this campaign by the actions and ambitions of secular governments, who brought their growing power to bear on the beliefs and behaviour of their subjects. Church and State were thus in alliance against the ethos of traditional religious practice.

Their efforts were not, however, assured of success. Popular religion derived quite naturally from contemporary economic and social conditions, especially in rural areas. Tridentine Catholicism, on the other hand, was consciously developed by celibates and intellectuals, men who belonged to a uniquely privileged group in society, and its prescriptions did not always match the expectations of the laity. Popular religion was essentially communal: in periods of fear and insecurity, individuals would gather together to perform agreed rituals to secure assistance against threats to the welfare of the whole group. The authorities' criticism of popular religion was therefore perceived in many cases as an attack on the community itself, and well-meaning attempts to eliminate local ceremonies were as a result often vigorously resisted by the laity.

To many Catholics, even in Europe, the Counter-Reformation must have seemed quite alien. We can see this most clearly, perhaps, when we examine the Church's plans to change the laity's understanding of morality. In several regions of France, it was common for all members of a family to sleep in one bed. In 1681, the Bishop of Grenoble tried to prevent this customary practice by ordering parents in his diocese not to sleep with their children: he was obviously anxious to eliminate the temptations of incest. But few peasant families could actually afford more than one bed, and the bishop's prohibitions were therefore bound to fail. Even where the reformers did seem to alter established patterns of behaviour, the consequences could be damaging. Before the Counter-Reformation, illegitimacy was not always considered a scandal, as long as the father was able and willing to support the mother and child financially. A rich man might find himself paying for several former mistresses and their children. There is no doubt that in some areas clerical opposition to concubinage during the Counter-Reformation had an effect on these attitudes, and so contributed to a decrease in the number of babies born out of wedlock: in the village of Pont-de-Vaux in Burgundy, the proportion of recorded illegitimate births dropped from over 5 per cent in the 1560s to less than 1 per cent in the 1670s. But it also encouraged less scrupulous men to repudiate their former lovers; deprived of male protection, these women were then often forced to leave the community, and to abandon or murder their children. Again, the preoccupations of the reformers did not always fit the realities of contemporary society.

It is not surprising, therefore, to discover that in many parts of Europe, the Counter-Reformation made only a limited impact. Sociologists and anthropologists in the twentieth century have recorded the retention in many countries of traditional customs derived from popular religion alongside orthodox Catholic rites and practices. In Andalusia, for example, the 'sabia', or wise woman, is still believed to be able to manipulate the powers of the spirit world for the benefit of the local community. There are plenty of examples of similar local figures in the records of the sixteenth and seventeenth centuries from several parts of Europe. Now, as in the past, they address their invocations to a mixture of Christian saints, pagan deities, and even material objects; their methods combine both natural and supernatural elements. Despite official opposition and the Church's teaching of 400 years or more, traces of the old popular religion have survived.

Outside Europe, the pre-conquest religions also survived, and the gap between Church and laity was even more obvious. Pastoral work was entrusted almost exclusively to Europeans, and Christianity was as a result often perceived as the religion of the conquerors, just one aspect of an alien racial and military domination. 'The God of the Christians does good for the Christians, but not for us', André Thevet was told by the Tupinamba of Brazil in the sixteenth century (Thevet, 1953, p. 264). The Church had difficulty uprooting polygamy and polyandry; in many areas, the missionaries complained that local people avoided them, and hid their children rather than allow the friars to educate them in Christian schools. Priests working with the Calchaquí of the lower Andes in Paraguay reported that their converts reverted to paganism as soon as the missionaries left the area: 'Not one of those, who had been formerly baptized, lived at this time like a Christian, but resided promiscuously among the heathens' (Del Techo, 1704, p. 722). In the seventeenth century, the ruler of Sundi in the Congo hid his pagan religious images in his house after his baptism, and continued to perform the traditional rituals in secret; in Mexico, the missionaries were horrified to discover that the Indians had hidden their ancient idols in the altars of Christian churches, so that they could worship their gods during Mass. Elsewhere, the new beliefs and rituals of Christianity were simply added to the old religion. In the later sixteenth century, Baltasar Ramírez wrote of the Peruvian Indians: 'They are not quite the idolators they used to be, nor are they quite the Christians we would like them to be. Limping, as it were, with both feet, they have recourse to both idolatry and Christianity' (Duviols, 1971, p. 349). In Senegal, in West Africa, baptized Catholics in the eighteenth century were found to be praying to Mohammed as well as Christ.

The popular devotion to the Virgin of Guadalupe at Tepeyac, in Mexico, may perhaps serve as a symbol of the tangled achievement of the Counter-Reformation. The cult now combines elements from the orthodox Catholic veneration of Mary, the Mother of Christ, with beliefs about the Aztec mother–goddess, Tonantzin, in whose sanctuary the Virgin appeared five times to an Indian convert in visions traditionally dated to 1531. 'It is clear', claimed the Franciscan Bernardino de Sahagún in his *Historia general de las cosas de la Nueva España*, written between 1558 and 1569, 'that in their hearts the common people who go [to Tepeyac] on pilgrimage are moved only by their ancient religion' (Lafaye, 1976, p. 217). This was a little harsh: the cult at Tepeyac was probably created out of a fusion of the

71

Aztec and the Spanish faiths. Christianity was selectively reinterpreted by the converts overseas – as it was in Europe – in terms that were consistent with the existing beliefs and rituals.

There were undoubtedly some genuine conversions, in Europe and abroad. It would be wrong not to mention the heroic resilience of the Japanese Catholic community during and after the horrifying persecutions that began in 1613: when missionaries were again permitted to travel in Japan, in 1865, they discovered that native Catholics had passed on their faith in secret from one generation to another, despite isolation and intolerance, for 250 years. But such examples were rare. The efforts of bishops, priests, missionaries, teachers, preachers, catechists and confraternities, resulted for the most part in a syncretic religion, in which traditional practices and ceremonies were combined with the Catholicism of Trent.

For all their virtues and their energy, the reformers of the Counter-Reformation were unable to resolve the dilemma which, in several different forms, has recurred throughout this short study. They were forced to choose between doctrinal probity and pastoral advantage. If they complied with the teaching of the Church, they might find themselves isolated from the laity; if they appeased the inclinations of the laity, they might violate the teaching of the Church. This is a dilemma which has troubled the Church at all periods of its history; but its bleak consequences became ever more apparent in the sixteenth and seventeenth centuries, as Catholicism reached out to the rural populations of Europe and the pagan populations overseas.

Guide to Further Reading

These notes are intended as an introductory guide to some of the books and articles in English which examine in more detail the themes discussed in this short study. For a more complete bibliography, see A. D. Wright, *The Counter–Reformation: Catholic Europe and the Non-Christian World* (London, 1982), pp. 295–327.

General

The standard account of Church history in this period is E. Iserloh, J. Glazik and H. Jedin, *Reformation and Counter-Reformation* (London, 1980), which is the fifth volume of the *History of the Church* edited by Jedin and J. Dolan. But the most innovative research has been influenced rather more by the subtle and illuminating survey of H. Outram Evennett, *The Spirit of the Counter-Reformation*, edited with a postscript by John Bossy (Cambridge, 1968), and by the radical interpretation of Jean Delumeau, *Naissance et Affirmation de la Réforme*, 2nd edn (Paris, 1968), and *Le Catholicisme entre Luther et Voltaire* (Paris, 1971). Unfortunately, only the second of Professor Delumeau's volumes has been translated, so the full scale of his reformulation is not easy for the English reader to grasp: *Catholicism between Luther and Voltaire: a new view of the Counter-Reformation*, with an introduction by John Bossy (London, 1977).

Michael Mullett, *The Counter-Reformation and the Catholic Reformation in early modern Europe* (London, 1984), provides an easy introduction to some of the debates, and A. D. Wright, *The Counter-Reformation: Catholic Europe and the Non-Christian World* (London, 1982), the fullest recent treatment, packed with ideas, but demanding for the beginner.

John Bossy, *Christianity in the West, 1400–1700* (Oxford, 1985), is a stimulating summary of the latest research, particularly valuable for its discussion of the contrast between medieval Christianity and the religion of the Protestant and Catholic reformers; for a lucid review, see Brendan Bradshaw, 'Utopia Lost', *The Times Literary Supplement*, 2 May 1986.

The best reference books are *The Oxford Dictionary of the Christian Church*, 2nd edn, ed. F. L. Cross and E. A. Livingstone (Oxford, 1974), and the *New Catholic Encyclopedia* (17 vols, New York, 1967, 1974, 1979).

Doctrine

For the early sixteenth-century interest in the problems of justification, see José C. Nieto, *Juan de Valdés and the Origins of the Spanish and Italian Reformation* (Geneva, 1970), and Dermot Fenlon's outstanding *Heresy and Obedience in Tridentine Italy: Cardinal Pole and the Counter Reformation* (Cambridge, 1972).

Peter Matheson, *Cardinal Contarini at Regensburg* (Oxford, 1972), examines the failure of the Conference of 1541.

The standard history of the Council is H. Jedin,

Geschichte des Konzils von Trent (4 vols, Freiburg, 1949–75); only the first two volumes have been translated into English: *A History of the Council of Trent* (2 vols, London, 1957–61). Professor Jedin's *Papal Legate at the Council of Trent: Cardinal Seripando* (St Louis, 1947) looks more closely at one of the leading figures of the early sessions, and his *Crisis and Closure of the Council of Trent: a retrospective view from the Second Vatican Council* (London, 1967) is a useful introduction to the later sessions.

For a good survey of the intellectual life of the period, see Robert Mandrou, *From Humanism to Science, 1480–1700* (Harmondsworth, 1978).

Alexander Sedgwick, *Jansenism in Seventeenth-Century France: voices from the wilderness* (Charlottesville, 1977), and more briefly Robin Briggs, 'The Catholic Puritans: Jansenists and Rigorists in France', in *Puritans and Revolutionaries: Essays in Seventeenth-Century History presented to Christopher Hill,* ed. Donald Pennington and Keith Thomas (Oxford, 1978), pp. 333–54, give a general account of Jansenism. The later period is covered by B. Robert Kreiser in *Miracles, Convulsions, and Ecclesiastical Politics in Early Eighteenth-Century Paris* (Princeton, 1978).

Giorgio de Santillana, *The Crime of Galileo* (New York, 1962), is still worth reading as an introduction to the arguments about astronomy. David Wootton, *Paolo Sarpi: between Renaissance and Enlightenment* (Cambridge, 1983), takes on the problem of atheism.

The clergy

Much of the recent research in English on diocesan and parochial reform has concentrated on Italy: O. M. T. Logan, 'The ideal of the Bishop and the Venetian Patriciate, *c.* 1430–*c.* 1630', *Journal of Ecclesiastical*

History, 29 (1978), pp. 415–50; C. Cairns, *Domenico Bollani, Bishop of Brescia: devotion to Church and State in the Republic of Venice in the sixteenth century* (Nieuwkoop, 1976); Christopher Black, 'Perugia and post-Tridentine church reform', *Journal of Ecclesiastical History*, 35 (1984), pp. 429–51; Thomas Deutscher, 'Seminaries and the education of Novarese parish priests, 1593–1627', *Journal of Ecclesiastical History*, 31 (1981), pp. 303–19.

On the Irish episcopate, see Donal F. Cregan, 'The social and cultural background of a Counter-Reformation episcopate, 1618–60', in *Studies in Irish History presented to R. Dudley Edwards*, ed. Art Cosgrove and Donal McCartney (Dublin, 1979), pp. 85–117. For France, see J. Michael Hayden, 'The social origins of the French episcopacy at the beginning of the seventeenth century', *French Historical Studies*, 10 (1977), pp. 27–40, and Richard M. Golden, *The Godly Rebellion: Parisian curés and the Religious Fronde, 1652–1662* (Chapel Hill, 1981), which examines the influence of Jansenism and Richerism on the clergy of Paris. On the situation in Spain, Henry Kamen, *Spain 1469–1714: a society of conflict* (London, 1983), especially pp. 177–90, and the same author's 'Clerical violence in a Catholic society: the Hispanic world, 1450–1720', *Studies in Church History*, 20 (1983), pp. 201–16.

Michael R. Weisser, *The Peasants of the Montes: the roots of rural rebellion in Spain* (Chicago, 1976), has some valuable remarks on the place of the Church in a peasant society.

H. O. Evennett, 'The New Orders', in *The New Cambridge Modern History*, vol. II, *The Reformation, 1520–59*, ed. G. R. Elton (Cambridge, 1958), pp. 275–300, is a helpful guide; Louis Ponnelle and Louis Bordet, *St Philip Neri and the Roman Society of His Times (1515–1595)*, (London, 1932) follows the career of the man who inspired the Italian Oratory.

For reform in the traditional monastic and mendicant orders, see V. Beltrán de Heredia, 'The beginnings of Dominican reform in Castile', in *Spain in the Fifteenth Century, 1369–1516*, ed. J. R. L. Highfield (London, 1972), pp. 226–47; P. J. S. Whitmore, *The Order of Minims in Seventeenth-Century France* (The Hague, 1967); A. J. Krailsheimer, *Armand-Jean de Rancé, Abbot of La Trappe: his influence in the cloister and the world* (Oxford, 1974).

The laity

There are now two useful surveys of lay attitudes: Peter Burke, *Popular Culture in Early Modern Europe* (London, 1978), and William Monter, *Ritual, Myth and Magic in Early Modern Europe* (Brighton, 1983).

For the religion which preceded the Reformation, see B. Moeller, 'Piety in Germany around 1500', in *The Reformation in Medieval Perspective*, ed. S. E. Ozment (Chicago, 1971); R. W. Scribner, 'Popular Religion in Catholic Germany at the time of the Reformation', *Journal of Ecclesiastical History*, 35 (1984), pp. 47–77; and L. Rothkrug, 'Popular Religion and Holy Shrines', in *Religion and the People, 800–1700*, ed. J. Obelkevich (Chapel Hill, 1979), pp. 20–86. The last volume has a very helpful introduction by the editor. For France, see A. N. Galpern, *The Religions of the People in Sixteenth-Century Champagne* (Cambridge, Mass., 1976), and Natalie Zemon Davis, 'The Sacred and the Body Social', *Past and Present*, 90 (1981), pp. 40–70. For Spain, the excellent books by William A. Christian, *Apparitions in Late Medieval and Renaissance Spain* (Princeton, 1981), and *Local Religion in Sixteenth Century Spain* (Princeton, 1981). For Italy, the influential works of Carlo Ginzburg translated by John and Anne Tedeschi: *The Night Battles: witchcraft and agrarian cults in the sixteenth and seventeenth centuries* (London, 1983), first published in Italian in 1966, and his more recent *The Cheese and the Worms: the cosmos of a sixteenth-century miller* (London, 1980), first published in Italian in 1976. Several of these studies – and especially those by Ginzburg – contain sections on the Catholic campaign against popular religion.

For the Church's efforts to build Catholic commitment, see Paul F. Grendler, 'The Schools of Christian Doctrine in sixteenth-century Italy', *Church History*, 53 (1984), pp. 319–31; John Bossy, 'Blood and Baptism: kinship, community and Christianity in Western Europe from the fourteenth to the seventeenth centuries', *Studies in Church History*, 10 (1973), pp. 129–43; and John Bossy, 'The Mass as a social institution, 1200–1700', *Past and Present*, 100 (1983), pp. 29–61.

On confession, compare the stimulating article by John Bossy, 'The social history of confession in the Age of the Reformation', *Transactions of the Royal Historical Society*, 25 (1975), pp. 21–38, with the debate between Thomas N. Tentler, Leonard E. Boyle and W. J. Bouwsma in *The Pursuit of Holiness in Late Medieval and Renaissance Religion*, ed. Charles Trinkaus with Heiko A. Oberman (Leiden, 1974), and with Professor Tentler's longer discussion, *Sin and Confession on the Eve of the Reformation* (Princeton, 1977).

Ronald F. E. Weissman, *Ritual Brotherhood in Renaissance Florence* (New York, 1982), examines confraternities. Brian Pullan, 'Catholics and the poor in early modern Europe', *Transactions of the Royal Historical Society*, 26 (1976), pp. 15–34, is clear and authoritative on poor relief.

The best introduction to the history of the family is probably M. Anderson, *Approaches to the History of the Western Family, 1500–1914* (London, 1980); Jean-Louis Flandrin, *Families in Former Times: kinship, household and sexuality* (Cambridge, 1979), uses examples from France to illustrate ecclesiastical attempts to reform family life.

A good summary of recent work on the Mediterranean Inquisitions is given in the review article of Geoffrey Parker, 'Some recent work on the Inquisition in Spain and Italy', *Journal of Modern History*, 54 (1982), pp. 519–32. Henry Kamen has now revised his account of the Spanish Inquisition: *Inquisition and Society in Spain* (London, 1985). The most recent thinking on the tribunal in Venice is provided by Brian Pullan, *The Jews of Europe and the Inquisition of Venice, 1550–1670* (Oxford, 1983). For other areas, see R. E. Greenleaf, *The Mexican Inquisition of the Sixteenth Century* (Albuquerque, 1969), and Alastair Duke, 'Salvation by Coercion: the controversy surrounding the "Inquisition" in the Low Countries on the eve of the Revolt', in *Reformation Principle and Practice: essays in honour of Arthur Geoffrey Dickens*, ed. Peter Newman Brooks (London, 1980), pp. 135–56. For the Middle Ages, Bernard Hamilton, *The Medieval Inquisition* (London, 1981).

Witchcraft, too, has received renewed attention in the past few years. For the gap between learned and popular conceptions, see Richard Kieckhefer, *European Witch Trials: their foundations in popular and learned culture, 1300–1500* (London, 1976); Sydney Anglo (ed.), *The Damned Art: essays in the literature of witchcraft* (London, 1977); and Norman Cohn, *Europe's Inner Demons* (London, 1975), which takes the story from Antiquity to the seventeenth century. A series of concise articles was published under the title 'The European Witchcraze revisited', with an introduction by Geoffrey Parker, in *History Today*, 30 (November 1980), pp. 23–39, and 31 (February 1981), pp. 22–36; the most recent work is Christina Larner, *Witchcraft and Religion: the politics of popular belief*, ed. with a foreword by A. Macfarlane (Oxford, 1984). Church and State are brought together by Bruce Lenman and Geoffrey Parker, 'The State, the

Community and the Criminal Law in early modern Europe', and Christina Larner, '*Crimen Exceptum*? The crime of witchcraft in Europe', in *Crime and the Law: the social history of crime in Western Europe since 1500*, ed. V. A. C. Gatrell, Lenman and Parker (London, 1980), pp. 11–48 and 49–75.

Missions

Examples of missions to Protestant areas are discussed in Oskar Garstein, *Rome and the Counter-Reformation in Scandinavia* (2 vols. Oslo, 1963–80), and Ian B. Cowan, *The Scottish Reformation: church and society in sixteenth century Scotland* (London, 1982). For recent debates on Catholicism in Anglican England, see E. Duffy, 'The English secular clergy and the Counter-Reformation', *Journal of Ecclesiastical History*, 34 (1983), pp. 214–30, and P. McGrath, 'Elizabethan Catholicism: a reconsideration', *Journal of Ecclesiastical History*, 35 (1984), pp. 414–28.

S. Neill, *A History of Christian Missions* (Harmondsworth, 1964), is a general account of missions overseas. C. R. Boxer, *The Church Militant and Iberian Expansion, 1440–1770* (Baltimore, 1978), is a remarkably learned and readable survey of research on the Spanish and Portuguese churches abroad; Anthony Pagden, *The Fall of Natural Man: the American Indian and the origins of comparative ethnology* (Cambridge, 1982), lucidly examines the theoretical debates about paganism and the pagans.

For more detailed examples of missionary work in different areas, see R. Ricard, *The Spiritual Conquest of Mexico: an essay on the apostolate and the evangelizing methods of the mendicant orders in New Spain, 1523–1572* (Berkeley, 1966); Charles Gibson, *The Aztecs Under Spanish Rule: a history of the Indians of the Valley of Mexico, 1519–1810*

(Stanford, 1964); I. Clendinnen, 'Disciplining the Indians: Franciscan ideology and missionary violence in sixteenth-century Yucatán', *Past and Present*, 94 (1982), pp. 27–48; John Leddy Phelan, *The Hispanization of the Philippines: Spanish aims and Filipino responses, 1565–1700* (Madison, Wis., 1959); James Axtell, *The European and the Indian: essays in the ethnohistory of colonial North America* (Oxford, 1981); D. G. Sweet and G. B. Nash (eds), *Struggle and Survival in Colonial America* (Berkeley, 1981); John D. Hargreaves, 'Assimilation in eighteenth-century Senegal', *Journal of African History*, 6 (1965), pp. 177–81; J. Gernet, *China and the Christian Impact: a conflict of cultures* (Cambridge, 1985); and C. R. Boxer, *The Christian Century in Japan, 1549–1650* (Berkeley, 1951).

Philip Caraman, *The Lost Paradise: an account of the Jesuits in Paraguay, 1607–1768* (London, 1975), tells the story of the Reductions in South America.

Georg Schurhammer, *Francis Xavier: his life, his times* (4 vols, Rome, 1973–82), is a massive study of the Church's most remarkable missionary.

The impact of the Counter-Reformation

On the survival of popular religion despite the Counter-Reformation, see (a few examples only) F. G. Vallee, 'Burial and mourning customs in a Hebridean community', *The Journal of the Royal Anthropological Institute of Great Britain and Ireland*, 85 (1955), pp. 119–30; Julian A. Pitt-Rivers, *The People of the Sierra*, 2nd edn (Chicago, 1971); João de Pina-Cabral, *Sons of Adam, Daughters of Eve: the peasant worldview of the Alto Minho* (Oxford, 1986); Jacques Lafaye, *Quetzalcóatl and Guadalupe: the formation of Mexican national consciousness, 1531–1813* (Chicago, 1976); and Peter Burke, 'Religion and Secularisation', in *The New Cambridge Modern History*, vol. XIII, *Companion Volume*, ed. Burke (Cambridge, 1979), pp. 293–317.

References

Abelly, Louis 1664: *La vie du venerable Serviteur de Dieu Vincent de Paul*. Paris.

Acosta, José de 1954: *Obras del P. José de Acosta de la Compañia de Jesus*, ed. F. Mateos. Madrid.

Alberigo, J. et al. (eds) 1962: *Conciliorum Oecumenicorum Decreta*. Freiburg.

Avenel, G. d' 1886: Le clergé français et la liberté de conscience sous Louis XIII. *Revue historique*, 32, 312–49.

Blair, Emma Helen and Robertson, James Alexander (eds) 1905: *The Philippine Islands, 1493–1898*, vol. 29. Cleveland, Ohio.

Bouchard, Gérard 1972: *Le village immobile: Sennely-en-Sologne au XVIIIe siècle*. Paris.

Boxer, C. R. 1951: *The Christian Century in Japan, 1549–1650*. London.

Boxer, C. R. 1975: *Mary and Misogyny: Women in Iberian Expansion Overseas, 1415–1815*. London.

Boxer, C. R. 1978: *The Church Militant and Iberian Expansion, 1440–1770*. London.

Buschbell, G. (ed.) 1916: *Concilium Tridentinum: Diariorum, actorum, epistolarum, tractatuum nova collectio*, vol. 10. Freiburg.

Certeau, Michel de 1965: Crise sociale et réformisme spirituel au début du XVIIe siècle: une 'nouvelle spiritualité' chez les Jésuites français. *Revue d'ascetique et de mystique*, 41, 39–86.

Chalumeau, G. 1958: Saint Vincent de Paul et les missions en France au XVIIe siècle. *XVIIe siècle*, 41, 317–27.

Croix, Alain 1981: *La Bretagne aux 16e et 17e siècles: la vie, la mort, la foi*, vol 2. Paris.

Del Techo, Nicholas 1704: The History of the Provinces of Paraguay, Tucuman, Rio de la Plata, Parana, Guaira and Urraica. In Awnsham and John Churchill (eds), *A Collection of Voyages and Travels*, vol. 4, London, 680–870.

Delumeau, Jean 1977: *Catholicism between Luther and Voltaire: a new view of the Counter-Reformation*. London.

Deyon, Pierre 1967: *Étude sur la société urbaine au 17e siècle: Amiens, capitale provinciale*. Paris.

Duvergier de Hauranne, Jean 1962: *Lettres inédites de Jean Duvergier de Hauranne, abbé de Saint-Cyran*, ed. A. Barnes, Paris.

Duviols, Pierre 1971: *La lutte contre les religions autochtones dans le Pérou colonial: 'L'Extirpation de l'idolâtrie' entre 1532 et 1660*. Paris.

Fenlon, Dermot 1972: *Heresy and Obedience in Tridentine Italy: Cardinal Pole and the Counter Reformation*. Cambridge.

François de Sales 1609: *Introduction à la vie dévote*. Lyon.

François de Sales 1617: *Traicté de l'amour de Dieu*. Lyon.

Galilei, Galileo 1934: *Le opere*, vol. 12. Florence.

Golden, Richard M. 1981: *The Godly Rebellion: Parisian Curés and the Religious Fronde, 1652–62*. Chapel Hill.

Gonçalves, Diogo 1955: *História do Malavar*, ed. J. Wicki. Münster.

Imberciadori, Ildebrandino 1959: Spedale, scuola e chiesa in popolazioni rurali dei secoli XVI–XVII. *Economia e storia*, 6, 423–49.

Jedin, Hubert 1947: *Papal Legate at the Council of Trent: Cardinal Seripando*. St. Louis.

Jedin, Hubert 1961: *A History of the Council of Trent*, vol. 2. London.

Lafaye, Jacques 1976: *Quetzalcóatl and Guadalupe: the Formation of Mexican National Consciousness, 1531–1813*. Chicago.

Le Comte, Louis 1696: *Nouveaux memoires sur l'État present de la Chine*, vol. 2. Paris.

Lenman, Bruce and Parker, Geoffrey 1980: The State, the Community and the Criminal Law in early modern Europe. In V. A. C. Gatrell, Lenman and Parker (eds), *Crime and*

the Law: the social history of crime in Western Europe since 1500,
London, 11–48.

Pagano, Sergio and Luciani, Antonio G. (eds) 1984: *I documenti
del processo di Galileo Galilei*. Vatican City.

Panigarola, Francesco 1592: *Prediche di Monsignor Reverendissimo
Panigarola Vescovo d'Asti*. Venice.

Pérouas, L. 1966: La pastorale liturgique au XVIIe siècle.
Mélanges de science religieuse, 23, 30–44.

Phelan, John Leddy 1959: *The Hispanization of the Philippines:
Spanish Aims and Filipino Responses, 1565–1700*. Madison.

Ponnelle, Louis and Bordet, Louis 1932: *St Philip Neri and the
Roman Society of his Times (1515–1595)*. London.

Ranke, Leopold von 1842: *The History of the Popes, their Church
and State, in the Sixteenth and Seventeenth Centuries*. London.

Rolle, Richard 1971: *The Fire of Love*. Harmondsworth.

Schurhammer, Georg 1982: *Francis Xavier: his life, his times*,
vol. 4: *Japan and China, 1549–52*. Rome.

Sedgwick, Alexander 1977: *Jansenism in Seventeenth-Century
France: Voices from the Wilderness*. Charlottesville.

Solórzano Pereira, Juan de 1648: *Política Indiana*. Madrid.

Thevet, André 1953: *Le Brésil et les Brésiliens*, ed. S. Lussagnet.
Paris.

Thwaites, Reuben Gold (ed.) 1898: *The Jesuit Relations and
Allied Documents*, vol. 23. Cleveland, Ohio.

Thwaites, Reuben Gold (ed.) 1900: *The Jesuit Relations and
Allied Documents*, vol. 60. Cleveland, Ohio.

85

Index

86

87